101 Ways
to Pick Stock
Market Winners

101 Ways to Pick Stock Market Winners

Clem Chambers

Beautiful
Books

Beautiful Books Limited
36-38 Glasshouse Street
London W1B 5DL

www.beautiful-books.co.uk

ISBN 9781907616273

9 8 7 6 5 4 3 2 1

Printed in the UK by CPI Mackays, Chatham ME5 8TD.

To my Father who taught me.

*For the millions of ADVFN users who look
to us to help build their prosperity.*

Introduction

Picking stocks need not be reserved for financial gurus and degree-wielding mathematicians in investment banks.

Picking good stocks just requires a toolbox of simple ideas that filter out and zero in on companies that investors should be looking to add to their portfolio, or traders should be looking to play.

Investing is not trading and visa versa. Investing is like farming, trading is betting. Both can be very lucrative and either can lose you your shirt.

However, in the main, investing is much easier, more leisurely and less risky. Investors might not get rich quick, but they shouldn't get poor fast either.

Investing is not necessarily that popular; whereas everyone likes to chance their arm at being a trading genius. It is, therefore, no wonder that the stock market carries a certain aroma of the casino.

Yet investing is the most prudent way to approach the market.

This guide carries investing and trading rules to help you select stocks for investing and trading.

They can be, and should be, combined to complement a stock selection, as while each can be the key to a stock selection, none are contradictory. The more of these rules fit the candidate the better.

The 101 ways are a series of techniques of which some are easy and some tricky, hence the difficulty rating. A difficulty of one would suggest the idea was simple even to a novice, and, win or lose, the choices to get in and out are very simple. A high score over five means the technique needs careful thought and might take a bit of reflection and practice to use. At the high end, an eight or nine rating would mean the technique was extremely tricky—a do or die method that should only be used if you are very confident.

The Long and Short of it.

The ways are also categorised by signal; either long or short (sometimes both).

When you buy a share you are long. That's simple enough to understand. Long means you own the share. If you have a thousand pounds of Shell, you are long a thousand pounds of Shell.

To be short is the opposite of long.

This idea can be confusing. How can you own minus a thousand pounds of Shell? How can you own negative shares? Well if you sell shares you don't have, you are short. This might sound illegal and wicked, but it is not and it is understood to be OK, even though people often moan about people who are short.

Shorting works like this:

You borrow some shares.

You sell them at a price to someone.

You buy them back and return them to the folks you borrowed them from.

When you go short, the broker arranges all the details, like borrowing etc, so you just sell and then buy back when you are done.

You sell and go short because you think a share will fall. If it falls you buy back cheaper than you sold and make a profit. If the share goes up and you buy it back you will have made a loss.

Picking stocks is not all about what makes a share good, it is also what makes a share bad and there are a few no-no rules that can melt the wings of any stock Icarus and dissuade an investor from getting involved.

To pick stock market winners you need the right tools. I use ADVFN, the website I am CEO of, as the platform to find the stocks I want to buy and sell. When I started ADVFN I put all my money into shares on the basis that this would guarantee my full attention on the tricky task of building a stocks and shares website that would actually be about growing a private investor's wealth rather than a pretty but vapid site driven by a bunch of graphic designers with 'no skin in the game'.

ADVFN is now a huge site with usage around the globe. It is

a leading site, not just in the UK, but in the US, Brazil and in various territories from Italy to Japan.

In essence this book is the condensation of my rules of thumb for investing and trading.

Amongst the ways, I have listed a few golden rules, which should be rigorously followed. Break them at your peril.

If you follow the principles listed in this book you should do rather well. Please feel free to send me a Christmas card when you do.

Don't be afraid to make up your own rules. If you think CEOs with beards can't be trusted then make it a rule and keep track of how it works. You may be right.

The thing to remember is there are 2000-plus stocks in the UK market, if you exclude one share there are still another 2000-plus to choose from. In any event you are going to ignore 99% of all possibilities, so developing your own rules is a useful way of winnowing the chaff.

As time passes you will build up your own toolkit of ideas and these will likely serve you well because experience is the most valuable asset of investment and it soon turns into your own valuable investment guidelines.

Golden Rule No. 1

Diversify

Do not put all your eggs in one basket. If you invest your money in too few shares you will not reap your just results.

If you put all your money into one share at a time, you risk losing the lot.

At best, if you do not diversify you will have a rough ride as the small number of shares in your selection buffet your capital around. Concentration of capital will not help your sleep.

Aim to own 30 stocks. If you do not have the capital to have 30, then build towards that number as you add money to your brokerage account.

Buy shares in units, say £1000, and do not increase your unit size until you have 30 stocks.

If you make £500 on a stock, the next share you buy should still be that £1000 unit, leaving the £500 aside until you have made up the extra to buy another stock at the £1000 unit size.

Always remember diversification is your best friend.

Internet chat rooms (discussion forums/ bulletin boards)

Not many people are cut out to be lonely hunters. Investors like to club together and discuss their positions. Internet chat rooms are unruly, garrulous places. They are like noisy medieval taverns; loud, uproarious and fun.

Is there gold to be had from the fetid river of free speech?

You bet.

Silence is golden

Signal: Long

Difficulty: 4

If you find that a discussion on a stock you are interested in is muted this is an extremely good sign.

People talk a lot about stocks when they are unsure or when they think their investment needs a shove in the right direction.

Solid stocks attract a solid kind of investor and while they like to communicate, they generally aren't the manic kind of people that inhabit many of the topics internet boards have to offer.

Successful investors are also likely to be well off and this again tends to keep the noise level down. They have little to prove and are merely dipping their toes into a board about a stock they own and have no desire to cause a fuss.

It takes a bit of time to get the hang of bulletin boards like ADVFN's, but once you've spent a few hours surfing, you will note how some threads are madness and some are sedate.

The more sedate the better.

Madness is badness

Signal: Short

Difficulty: 7

When you find a share which is the topic of furious debate on a bulletin board, whatever you do, do not buy it. The noisier the thread, the more virulent the language, the more colourful the debate, the worse the prospects are for the company.

Dying companies attract the attention of the worst investors. They are like lemmings to a cliff.

There is some justification for this, as a disastrous stock has a tiny chance of making a Lazarus-like return and if this does happen its share price will rocket.

This 100 to one chance of making ten times your money is what attracts the stock trader moths to the flame. To them the attraction of a possible ten times profit dwarfs the fear engendered of losing 99 times in a row to get one fat win.

If you are plucky, you will short the stock and watch the spectacle of dozens of dizzy stock gamblers lose their shirts.

However it's a tricky game, best only played for pennies. There are more sensible ways to make money.

Way 3

'Due dil'

Signal: Long or Short

Difficulty: 4

Bulletin Boards are a great place to get the background story on a company. Quite often people discussing stocks will have a good knowledge of what the real story is behind a company. Whether it's a crazy discussion about a risky stock or a boring one, a lot of detail and history will be on display. Merely reading a discussion that has taken place over a number of years will give a good flavour of what has and is going on behind the headlines. This can be invaluable when you are sizing up a share for its inner personality in your selection process.

You can't do too much 'due diligence', and a message board thread can be like having lunch at the work's canteen.

Locate minnows

Signal: Long

Difficulty: 6

There are over 2000 stocks on the UK market. Unless you have all the time in the world and the memory of an elephant, there is no way you can know all the companies trading on the stock exchange.

There are many ways of zeroing in on the interesting ones and a good one is internet chat rooms. Without doubt there is a lot of bad information about poor companies but that shouldn't put you off. After a while searching for companies, you know roughly what you are looking for. However, that does not necessarily mean you can find all the candidates right away.

Untold investors and traders are doing what you are doing and once they have found a stock they then try to tell everyone, so that their 'friends' will help drive the price up. There is nothing wrong with that, particularly as it's an opportunity to have a prospect added to your pick list.

You have to be very choosy of course and go off and do your research, but a stock discussion is a good place to find names to add to the hopper of new candidates.

There are many small companies. Any company with a market cap less than £250 million is considered small. But small can mean £10 million. These micro caps can be great companies but they can also be rubbish. The gems are in amongst the tailings. Bulletin Boards are a good place to go sieving for these gems as, in the main, no one covers these companies with broker research. Bulletin Board chat is a quick way to browse the micro-cap world to home in on companies worth further research. It's a good jumping off point in the high risk world of small cap investing.

Stock charts and technical trading

It's been proven that share charts do not tell the future, yet all investors use them. Many simply couldn't trade or invest without them. It is true that if you pour over all the data of minute or day scale moves for shares, it's nearly impossible to find a scheme that robotically makes money. This is because this ore has long since been mined out.

When looking at the data it all appears pretty random.

What follows are ways I pick stocks using charts. Unsurprisingly, these are novel ideas. There will always be new ways to make money using charts and over time they will stop working. This is the way it is with markets. By telling you I may be responsible for killing my own techniques. Hopefully the book will have to sell bucket loads for this to happen.

Also, to be successful you need to be constantly on the look out for new methods; old ones are always eaten away by the efficient market. To make gold you must slowly destroy your philosopher's stone and then make another.

(Note: Don't believe chart examples. Only ones that work are ever shown. Mine of course are an exception to this rule: not. My examples are to illustrate the idea and are not in anyway proof.)

Good horses on steady courses

Signal: Long/Short

Difficulty: 7

Volatility is a measure of how much a share ducks and dives in the course of its trading. Volatility is a technical manifestation of uncertainty. If the market hasn't got a good handle on the future value of a stock, its view will swing about in a bipolar way. This uncertainty means volatility.

So, as an outsider, a quick look at the performance of a stock over a period will give you a quick view of whether the market knows what is going on.

If you put money in your bank deposit, the graph of your money will go up very smoothly. If a stock is rising or falling smoothly, you can be assured that for now the market feels comfortable with the current trend.

Conversely, if the day-to-day action is all over the place the market has no idea how to price the share.

This means a rising stock with low volatility is a strong bet, while putting money into a volatile stock can be seen as a WAG (Wild Arsed Guess).

So, if you liked a stock and it was going up in a smooth way, it's another good indication this is a good selection.

To add to this idea, a stock that has fallen and then gone into a long period of sideways trading with low volatility is a candidate for recovery. The bad news would seem to be out of the system and the share forgotten. This is another nice set up for a long.

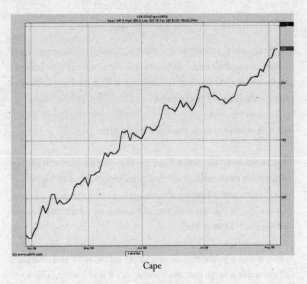

Cape

Not much uncertainty here as Cape makes lucky buyers, like myself, a good post crash profit.

Dud IPOs

Signal: Short

Difficulty: 6

For many years now IPOs (Initial Public Offerings) have been infrequent and variously over-priced. It's a vicious circle: an IPO is launched onto the UK market; it falls and puts everyone off for the next one. Not like Tell Sid days.

It is a rare IPO that doesn't fall badly after launch.

This is because the bank floating the company is relying on its position as an important financial supplier to stuff pension funds with over-priced shares. It's a racket, and like all rackets spoils the market and dissuades a vibrant market for new issues. C'est la vie.

What is does mean is you can short a UK IPO and watch it fall away for a fat profit. As I write, it's a no brainer. The only thing to watch out for is a big pre-IPO cut in the IPO price. If this happens then perhaps the price will be right and there will be a post-IPO rise. However if the IPO is uneventful the after market is liable to sag.

By the time you read this it will be a good idea to research the last six to 12 IPOs and see how they did. If this scheme is still holding true, why wouldn't you short the next IPO?

This is of course trading. As such it's more tricky than

good old investing.

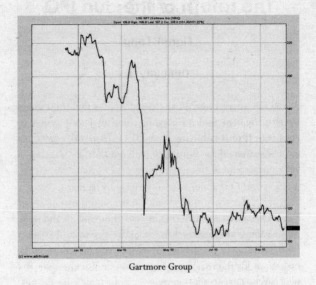

Gartmore Group

Gartmore. Your pension funds bought this dud, no doubt. See Way 7 for what to do next.

The return of the dud IPO

Signal: Long

Difficulty: 6

A dud IPO doesn't mean the company is a dud. You could say that the bank which floats the company is responsible to stick it to investors buying in the IPO. The bank represents the old shareholders wanting to bail, not the new wanting to get a piece of the action.

Post-IPO, the share will flounce down and down, another bum IPO... But stocks don't go down forever in the same way as they don't go up forever. After a year or two they hit a bottom and are poised for a bounce. This can often be because it has taken a year or two for the various new and old shareholders to get themselves comfortable with the new set up. When the share hits bottom, it's a good candidate for adding to your portfolio. As with all these ways, you can use them on their own or better still combine them for a more rigorous selection process.

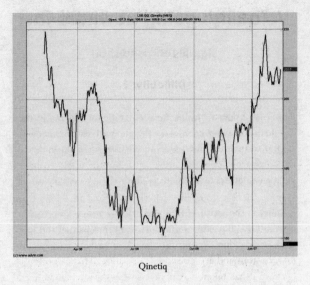

Qinetiq

Qinetiq bounces back from its post-IPO fall. It then fell off again…

Volatility: going nowhere fast

Signal: Long and short

Difficulty: 7

Everyone wants to know how to trade, when really they should be longing to invest. People will swap money for excitement any day, which is not what they set out to do.

Swing trading is a favourite trading theme. What you are looking for is a company that flails around in a long-term channel—say between 80p and 100p—every few months. The idea is you go long at the bottom of the channel and short at the top of the channel as the share price rattles around going nowhere fast.

If you want to experience the thrill of riding this particular tiger, then the key is to build up a universe of stocks behaving in this way and then pick only the best ones to play with. The key to trading is only backing the blindingly obvious while leaving the rest. To do this (and not go crazy waiting around) you have to have a big selection of games waiting to be played. Then there is a chance that of the 30 or 40 situations, one will stare out at you as a no brainer.

Otherwise you will be trading half chances and making your broker rich.

With swing trading there is much scope for picking stocks to keep an eye on. To find them just pull up five year charts, which can be found on ADVFN, of the top 300 stocks. Candidates will stand out.

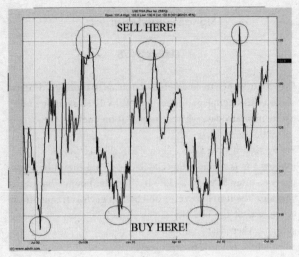

RSA Insurance

RSA has been choppy and range bound for years. The last sell point in retrospect sub-sequentially looks high risk as rumours of takeovers push its price up to the top of the range. Selling at the top and buying at the bottom takes nerves!

Dead cat bounces

Signal: Long

Difficulty: 8

Most trading courses will tell you to avoid trading a dead cat bounce like the plague. They say: 'Why catch a falling knife?' Why indeed. The reason is simple: as no one else does, there is money to be had.

When a stock takes a big knock due to a piece of bad news it very often falls off a cliff. It will then bounce back a bit because the initial panic caused by this news is frequently an over-reaction.

The idea is to catch the recovery.

This is how you do it:

Don't catch the falling knife. Wait for it to hit the ground, then wait for a day or two, then buy in.

The delay changes with market conditions, so it is always a good idea to keep track of collapsing shares and measure the delay from slump to bump. Then, with this in mind, you can get in for the dead cat bounce. The key is to bail as soon as it has bounced for two or three days. While some bounces can keep going, many roll over and collapse again.

The key is to only trade solid companies rather than inherently risky ones. However once you have tried the scheme on good companies you can stretch your reach a little.

Unlike easy investing gambits, trading a dead cat bounce is tricky. It takes nerve, patience and discipline. As a high risk/reward trade you should keep your position as a tiny proportion of your capital. It takes no time at all to blow your money trading. If you want to attempt the advanced trading stuff, take it slow and keep your education inexpensive.

Gartmore Group

This dead cat was thrown from high up and bounced a lot. You had to be quick to get out if you dared catch it.

Buy the Bull

Signal: Long

Difficulty: 5

A Bull market makes everyone a genius. Any fool can buy in a Bull market and make money. Likewise a genius who is long in a Bear market will lose money. As such, knowing what market you are in is the key.

It's a simple call, but if you want to make an expert sweat ask him if the market is going up or down. You don't have to be wimpy like this, you can ask yourself: Is the market going up or down?

If you don't know, why are you investing?

Personally, I think we are on the edge of a very long-term Bull, but that shouldn't influence you.

If you think this too, you can just buy a FTSE tracker and forget about it for 20 years. You'll likely be very happy with the results after this time.

Likewise you could pick 30 stocks you fancy and look at them once a year and do a tidy up. This will look a lot like the FTSE tracker return, but if you are good at picking you may beat it. This is likely to be better than you would have got in the bank.

You can of course put your brain to work and with a bit of luck get good at investing and do a lot better than a FTSE tracker.

The key thing is to know the market is Bullish, because investing against a head wind is tough work.

The thing about a Bull or a Bear market is the window. If you are looking to invest for two to three years look at the long-term chart. Here is a long-term chart. Which way do you think it goes next?

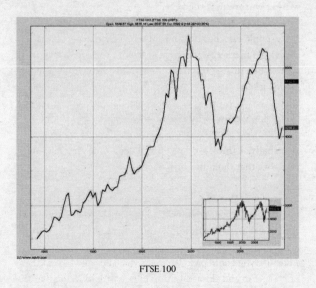

FTSE 100

This is the FTSE 100, summer 2008, shown quarterly. Yes, it went up about 30% from this point to the time of writing.

Know the general market trend

There is a lot of rubbish talked about stocks. The real question is: Is the stock or market going up or down? If you don't know, don't play, whether you are trading for a minute a day or investing for ten years.

A Bear market is not after a market has fallen 20%. It is when it is falling in a trend—regardless of how much it has fallen.

A Bull or a Bear market is when the tendency for that market is in a general upwards or downwards direction over an extended period of time. This can be for the next five minutes, five days or five years.

A long-term Bull market will be peppered with many short-term Bear phases.

As such, you need to look at your investment time horizon. If you are investing for three years, you don't care about a two month Bear phase. If you were trading a stock for a week, you most certainly would. Match your view of market direction with your investment horizon.

I say the market is going up over the next 10 years and that my two-to-five year investment timeline fits in nicely with that. As such I was happy to sit through May 2010's big correction without too much bitterness. As I write, in September 2010, it is already leaving the system and by mid next year will be all but forgotten. I say it's going up, between now and whenever, and that is why I'm long.

If you can't identify the trend of your investment time horizon, don't get involved. Trading or investing without a view backed by knowledge is random behaviour and the costs of doing so will consume all your money over time.

If you can't answer the obvious question, is it going up or down, then that is an answer in itself. You can't lose your shirt watching and waiting from the sidelines. When you know, it's time to play.

Sell a Bear

Signal: Short

Difficulty: 4

The market is symmetrical. Just like in physics, if something works one way the opposite will work the other way. So you could write Way 10 in the negative and it would work just as well. Rather than do that, I will explain a way to know when you are in a Bear phase. In a Bear phase, a little bad news will smash prices, while a little good news won't move prices at all. So if you flip this around for a Bull, you will see that a bit of bad news will be ignored while a bit of good news will send prices zooming.

In a Bear market a chimp can short and get rich, while a good stock picker will flounder.

As stated in Way 10, knowing the market bias is the starting point. Theory says you can't know this but you can get a feeling for it.

Another sign is the shape of the chart wave of a Bull and Bear. In a Bear market, prices spike then drift off and in a Bull they slump and then drift back up. The sharp move of the Sawtooth is actually the opposite of the market bias.

This might feel wrong but one of the reasons people hang on in against the trend is the series of near escapes that give them hope. When you pull away to the long-term, these short-term moves disappear and the trend is shown.

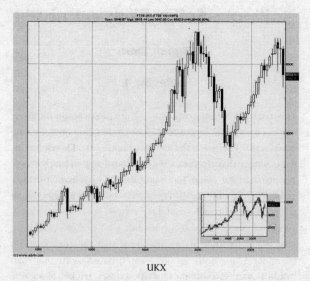

UKX

The FTSE 100 during the beginning of the credit crunch. Once again, the long-term view comes to the rescue.

Selling a Bull, selling a bubble

Signal: Short

Difficulty: 8

Everyone has amazing hindsight. To those who go on about the dotcom boom or the credit bubble as being obvious, you should ask how much they made shorting it. The answer is inveterately that they made none. Today as I write there are several bubbles: China for instance. The idea that China is a bubble is held only on the fringes. To me it's a bubble that at some time will burst.

The trouble with shorting bubbles is that they can keep on going for a long time. A bubble can inflate way further than you'd guess. So shorting a bubble is very tricky. However, bubbles do not deflate overnight.

Rather than try and get in at the top, the best thing to do is wait until the fall is well under way then jump on board. The dotcom bubble took two years to deflate and the credit crunch kicked off in 2007; almost a year before the final crash. So leaving the bubble to come unstuck is a good idea because although you might lose the bragging rights of catching the top and perhaps a few percentage points, you will lower the risk of the bubble continuing and hurting you.

Also the maths is in your favour. Say the top was 100 and the bottom was going to be 25. If you shorted at 100 and closed at 25, you'd make 75% of your money. If you shorted at 50 and sold at 25 you still make 50% of your money. For lots of complicated reasons you could argue this doesn't help, but if you are sure you are dealing with a bubble, it does. Bubbles very seldom re-inflate, so once a bust is established, it is a one-way bet. Nevertheless, playing bubbles is a tricky business but it is a lucrative one.

A good sign a bubble has blown is an initial period of silence, when the market and media seem not to have noticed that the bubble market is falling. This is a signal that all the longs are in denial. They are of course utterly committed and unable to buy more, so when the rollercoaster comes off the tracks there is often a period of silence, before the screams kick off.

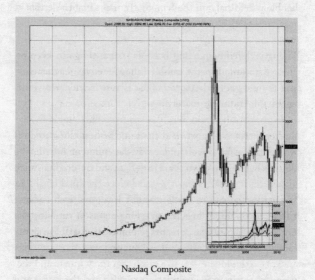

Nasdaq Composite

The Tech bubble in all its glory. The small chart shows it in relation to the Dow.

Buying a Bear, buying a crash

Signal: Long

Difficulty: 7

A crash is an amazing event in any market. It is pure adrenaline and high drama. Fortunes are made and lost but generally lost. When markets crash there is a superb opportunity to pick up good stocks cheap. In a crash everything falls and there is little discretion. At the end of the process positions can be added that give enormous returns after the crash is over.

Buying a crash is like selling a bubble and, once again, it is best to leave it until after the crash has happened to get in rather than try and get the bottom as the collapse is underway. The bigger the crash the more post-event time you have to get in. Proper crashes very rarely recover quickly and it is said one year is quick. So when the balloon goes up it is time to go looking for bargains rather than the moment to jump in willy-nilly.

Normally what causes the bust is not what you want to buy. It's the companies dragged down for no reason you want to buy. When the market crashes, companies that have been around forever will be crushed alongside all those bubble stocks that imploded. It is in a crash that the winners and the losers are separated. The winners survive and the losers are shown for what they are: puffed up confections with no solid business under the hood.

While you are making your post-crash selections do not listen to the media. They will be prophesying the end of the financial world. They are wrong again, it still isn't.

Just look at the balance sheet of the companies you are interested in and grab the ones beaten down but with solid assets and business. When the panic is over they will come good, while the weak companies go under.

UKX

Starting to slowly buy after the initial bust in 2008 was a very lucrative strategy. You could have held off to the bottom in March but that would have needed much more luck than judgement. The big chart shows the period between late 2007 and March 2009 that is highlighted in an oval in the small chart at the bottom left of the picture.

Investing in the Bull, trading in the Bear—buying the dips

Signal: Long

Difficulty: 5

'Buying the dips' is a classic long-term investors' trick. Of course anyone can make money buying in a Bull market and sitting tight. The whole point about knowing you are in a Bull is that it leaves you free to operate with confidence. However, once you are onto a good thing, the question is how to optimise your returns. Of course there are a million and one ways to lose even in the jaws of victory, but sticking to the golden rules should protect you. Therefore it is finding tricks to increase your returns that can make a big difference to your long-term outcome.

One way to optimise your returns is to buy when the market falls within the Bull run; a little Bear inside of a big Bull.

Nothing goes straight up in the market. All prices have a fair amount of down zag for every upward zig. If you save your buying for the downward zags this can help your returns.

A portfolio is a great help in this if you have already spread your money, because you can top up on shares when they drop, and because you have a basket to choose from there is always one stock sagging down at any one time. That way your money doesn't sit idly by waiting for a whole market correction.

Investing in the Bear, trading in the Bull—selling the rallies

Signal: Short

Difficulty: 5

It is important to remember the idea of market symmetry. If buying the dips works in a Bull, selling the rallies works in a Bear. It has to because if the market wasn't symmetrical, an infinite number of one way bets would develop which everyone could make money from. That would be nice, but it would have the effect of draining all the money out of the market and killing it. Again, it's the same as physics; if physics were asymmetrical the universe would break. Imagine if the same amount of effort moved you along one dimension further than the other…well pretty soon we'd all be stuck down one end of the universe. In a sense, profit in investing is about finding asymmetries because by trading them you push the market back into balance. In a way this is what the market pays you to do; make it efficient and symmetrical.

So, 'selling a rally in a Bear' is just the reverse of buying the dips in a Bull. They key is knowing what market you are in.

Flat-lining companies: dead or in a coma?

Signal: Long

Difficulty: 7

Unless you are looking at an index, which by its nature is a heavily traded instrument, after a crash in a stock there will be a period of long-term inactivity.

This inactivity is a long-term recovery period that a good company which has had bad luck will suffer.

When companies crash, the ones that go on to collapse normally continue their collapse pretty quickly after their first catastrophic blow. This is because they are a 'pack of cards'. A knock sets the whole thing cascading out of control. Conversely, a solid business will likely recover its poise after a long period of recuperation and then start off on a recovery.

As such, splitting the wheat from the chaff after a stock has slumped involves watching and waiting.

A company with a long-term flat line is an interesting candidate to look into further. If there is a solid business under the hood of a company that has crashed and then flat lined for an extended period of time it could be about to enjoy a renaissance. These are exactly the sort of companies you want to own shares in.

Hornby

Going nowhere until…

Volume rises

Signal: Long

Difficulty: 7

A long time ago it was noticed that a sleepy share would suddenly develop a strong growth in trading volume before its price would rocket up. This was because the insiders were buying on secret information that good news was on the way. This led to the belief that a sudden rise of volume was a prelude to good news.

This is of course no less true today than in the past, even with all the laws to stop this kind of skulduggery; after all insider trading is criminal. A sudden rising volume is an interesting indicator that something is afoot and is still regularly evident in the markets despite greater stringency from the authorities

However, the story might be different.

Rising volume is often used to lure traders into a stock; it's a fat worm to a greedy trout. The bait of rising volume suggests that something is afoot when actually it isn't and is just a trap.

'Wash trading', where someone buys and sells to themselves is a way to fake volume. Using this method a fraudster can create a sudden rise in volume in a dodgy stock and traders are lured in to buy. This trap is set because someone actually wants to sell. There is no news coming, just a loss to any trader suckered in.

This is the core of 'pump and dump'– a way shady operators make money by skinning unwary traders.

Yet in big stocks which cannot be so easily manipulated, a rising volume is a sign the trend is in place and likely to go further. An increase in popularity should, and does, raise the price of a share.

However, at the extremes, rules of investing tend to flip upside down. The very end of a trend is often shown by a climax in volume. In this case the investor will see an explosion of volume and a dramatic price rise. This climax of volume is the closing move and suggests a finale is reached. As such a huge increase in volume can indicate the end of the game.

(Of course laws of symmetry apply here too. A crash is often ended with what is known as 'a puke' when vast volumes of selling make a bottom.)

But strong rising volume is not the same as the huge volume marking a market limit. It's the difference between a gale and a hurricane.

Buying BS when the Bull rules

Signal: Long

Difficulty: 8

When markets are hot, good companies and bad companies all rise up together. The market often loses its efficiency at the limits of its range. This is why bubbles make billion dollar valuations of poor companies. However, soon enough normality is restored and it is tricky to play the extremes.

However, if you are in such a period there is opportunity for big profits. Near the end of a big Bull trend, all the rubbish at the bottom of the market will boom. It's an avalanche set off by other weak companies suddenly shooting up. Suddenly all the dross in a portfolio will come alive and, seeing this, investors will look for similar companies. As these companies are small and thinly traded their prices will rocket and, so long as you don't have too much to sell, you can make a tidy profit.

This is an aggressive tactic and one that should be marginal for your overall strategy, however next time you are in the last legs of a bubble be ready to trade some crazy stocks. It's what traders call 'option money', as if you lose you won't care too much, but if you win the returns are sweet enough to add a little extra overall return.

Boxing clever

Signal: Long or Short

Difficulty: 6

When shares really take off there is a lot at stake: huge profits or lost opportunity. Without hindsight it is hard to know when to hold or fold when a stock is rocketing.

It would be impossible to even try to judge without a stock chart, but even with one it is hard to know what to do.

Back in 1960 a speculator called Nicolas Darvas wrote a book called *How I Made $2,000,000 in the Stock Market*. His main trick was to put a box around a share's trading level and use the top and bottom bound to indicate whether the rise was over or not.

If the price broke through the upper bound of the box it was a buying signal, if it broke through the bottom it was a selling signal.

It's primitive but effective and certainly helps the investor or trader have a stop loss system which is easy to follow.

What is happening is a share 're-prices.' This means the market suddenly concluded a share should trade at a different level, because of a change in factors. This new price, say 100 now rather than 50 previously, is a new level the share will oscillate around. This oscillation after time establishes a spot the market considers roughly the right value for the company. If something new crops up, the market will re-price again either upwards or downwards. Putting a box around the new level defines the random shaking around the new levels and if that range is broken, something new is happening.

Like all systems, you should be loathed to use it alone. You need to be cynical, clinical and focused to make any tool work in stocks. Nonetheless, when a stock you hold goes into flight or free fall, putting a box around the new level is a good way of putting limits around your position and giving yourself clear guidelines on whether it is time to buy or sell.

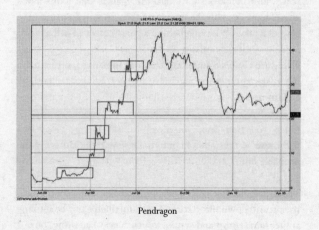

Pendragon

Boxing practice.

Rockets. Ladles of money

Signal: Long or Short

Difficulty: 8

It's a sad fact that most people who buy this book don't want to get rich slowly, they want to make an overnight fortune playing the markets. Sadly it's not that easy.

The stock that everyone wants to pick is the one that goes up 1000%. If you are determined to go looking for these then you need to look out for a chart formation that looks like a bowl forming, with the hope that the cup will form into the base of a take off leaving behind a chart pattern I call a ladle.

There are always companies that form this shape, often in the speculative end of the market of the day, be that technology or mining.

Once you find one, you need to use the previous box technique to try and hold onto the rise without suffering the probable fall.

The stock market is littered with stocks that go up like a rocket and down like a stick. Catching them early by looking at the right sectors and contenders in them, then using 'boxes' to try and avoid missing the upside while avoiding the downside, is the way to go. But it is a very tricky combination, which is why if you get it right, it pays so well.

One of the overarching rules of investing, which should always be born in mind: Risk = reward and often risk = stress.

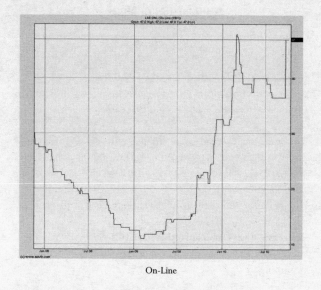

On-Line

A typical chart pattern of an explosively rising stock.

Risk = reward

People like to think they can get so good at trading and investing that they make their money from being right.

Sadly that's probably not the case.

The market pays you to participate.

The market pays you to take risk; the risk of holding shares is that you might lose your money. The way companies are funded means they need to sell shares and reward the consequent shareholder for their participation. The higher the chance of a problem, the more shareholders need to be paid to pony up.

This is why risk = reward.

Your smarts as an investor can add to your returns, but risk will always be the base reason why you are getting paid so having as many ways to control risk as possible is a good idea. Then you can take on more, make more returns and not suffer catastrophe.

Half way or whole way

Signal: Long or Short

Difficulty: 8

There is a core principle underpinning the market. This is the efficient market hypothesis. In a nutshell it maintains the market and is very good at pricing shares, so that by and large shares are the right price. Consequentially day-to-day price changes are random.

Everyone in the market laughs at this idea, but not many laugh all the way to the bank. In fact the people that follow the truth that the market is highly efficient are generally the ones making the money.

For instance, a broker is happy for you to invest in the market and facilitate you doing so for a tiny commission, but appears less than keen to jump in the game themselves. This maybe why brokers go on forever yet traders seldom last long. This makes perfect sense from an 'efficient markets' point of view. Better a commission today than the hope of a profit tomorrow.

How does this help us pick stocks? The key is random: the market is random. Now I won't bore you with facts or proofs and I apologise to pedantic math-types for the following hand wavy explanations of one way random can help you.

There are plenty of different types of random and let's

not examine that.

However, in some cases the following is true. If you are on a journey of a very random kind, you are likely to be half way through it at any given moment on a 50/50 chance basis.

This can mean if you have written one book, you are 50/50 likely to write two, and if you have written ten you are 50/50 likely to write 20 in total. The further you go on, the further you are likely to go on. You will drop dead at some point and then the process will end, but we know intuitively that the more you do, the more you end up doing. The rich get richer etc.

It is one of those crazy probability phenomena that you think can't work but that have a habit of doing so.

This idea is useful when a stock suddenly goes off a cliff or rallies. How far will it go? After the first move it will settle down and then the question is: Where to now?

The answer time and again is: it's either gone half way or the whole way.

This is particularly useful when combined with the previous 'box' techniques because when a stock hits an equilibrium point you can use Way 21 to set the boundaries needed to be broken to give you the answer.

This might sound like hedging your bets and in a good way it is, because it's a 50/50 bet with a much better payout than the odds. This is because if you are half way, you don't need much of a signal to give you an insight into a big upside, likewise you don't have to hold a stock all the way down, when the 'half way or whole way rule' suggests the fun is over.

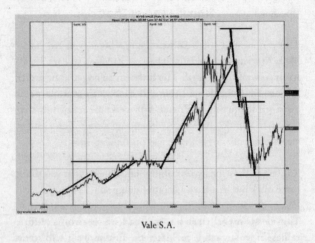

Vale S.A.

This is Vale, a huge Brazilian miner. Boxes and half-way analysis could help Brazilians make millions.

Long-term levels

Signal: Long or Short

Difficulty: 8

Charts aren't necessarily much use in telling the future. If they were, we'd all get rich very quickly. They are however very good at telling you the past.

Sadly hindsight doesn't have a great reputation.

However there is a use for hindsight.

Take a company that has been bumbling along minding its own business for ten years. It hasn't set the world on fire; it hasn't grown more or less than anyone else. Like most companies, for all its efforts, nothing much happened to it as a business.

However, the price has been all over the place as the share has traded through boom and bust and back again. One year its sector was in vogue yet five years later the sector was just not the place to be for institutions. This has a big impact on the share price.

What happened to the intrinsic value of the business over that period? Nothing.

However, the actual value the market assigned to the company was all over the place during that period. This is where a smart investor makes good money. The market pays you to be sensible, not a follower of fashion.

You like the stock but you want to know if it's cheap or expensive. Quite a lot of companies with these characteristics will suggest a price level where the company belongs, so that if a crash or some other emergency has struck, you can see where, given enough time, the company might recover to. By looking at the chart you can spot places where the company traded in a narrow range for a long period. A quick snapshot should give you an idea of a range of value the market was happy for the company to have in the past. These give a steer to valuations for the company in normal circumstances. This is particularly useful in booms and busts when things get out of whack, but as for markets so for sectors and as for sectors so for individual stocks.

This is also a good indicator of a target price for companies that have had to dilute their shareholders with the sales of new shares to raise money to save their bacon. That happened a lot in the credit crunch.

Say a company was trading happily at 400p before the emergency struck, then suddenly had to dilute by a big rights issue so that there are now four times as many shares. That would mean its zone of comfort should be at about £1 (400p/4). Roughly speaking, the company should be worth the same as it was before, only now its balance sheet is fatter.

However, chances are it will be trading at 65p after all the chaos. Unless something new and nasty comes along, given time, the share will recover to the £1. As an investor, it's just a case of being happy a healing process is underway.

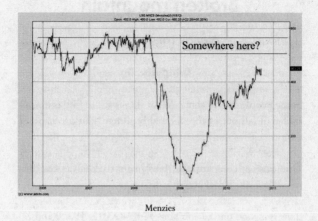

Menzies

*This chart is highly suggestive of the company's share price once
normality returns. Having said that, I personally sold most at around
the latest levels shown. I did, however, buy it at the lows and greed
never overcomes fear when I have a very fat profit.*

Broken mountain

Signal: Long or Short

Difficulty: 8

Some people like to short. What they want to find is a stock that will fall out of the sky and bag them a fat profit doing so.

One type of company that falls like a stick is the one that once flew like a rocket upwards.

This is a good one to combine with Ways 12, 19, 20 and 21. As always, the more rules that fit the share the better.

A share has gone off like a space shuttle and then plateaus. The longer the plateau goes on for the more likely a decisive break down will indicate the end of an era for the stock.

Some people will call this a head and shoulders but frankly I can never see the head and this 'broken mountain' form doesn't often have the middle section suggested to be the head.

My view is simply the obvious: The share shot up…hit an equilibrium level…stuck there…then fell away. It could happen on a small range, it can happen on a big scale. However, when it happens big time, the reversion to old price levels is very tasty for a shorter.

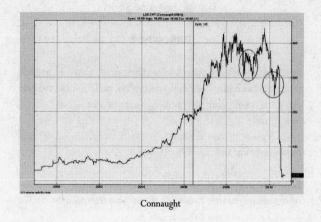

Connaught

Death of a company.

Way 24

The Big U

Signal: Long

Difficulty: 8

Let's stick with the idea of equilibrium. A share is happily trading in a channel of equilibrium. The progress is a neutral range of zigzagging. If nothing changes this would go on indefinitely.

However, nothing sits still.

Someone drops a piano on the Chairman's head. The price of the share craters; it dibbles about for a few months until a new Chairman establishes themselves.

The market is reassured and up the price goes to where it was.

Once you see the second leg of the U in place, it's an easy long.

Pianos are not the only thing to cause this behaviour; it might be a major shareholder needing to sell out for any one of a number of random reasons. A big block of stock will dig a crater in the price and when the overhang is gone, the price will float back up again. The same principle can be seen at work intraday on stocks. An institution selling a couple of million pounds of stock can bite a short-term hole in a stock that will take hours to repair. Like most things in the market, symmetry applies not only in terms of market direction but also in scale and time.

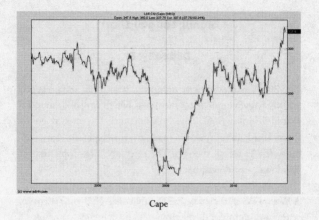

Cape

This chart of Cape demonstrates how an outside, one off incident takes a bite out of the share price. It also neatly demonstrates the values of Way 22 as the long-term level is regained. You can also see the mark of the next way—'The Big W'.

The Big W

Signal: Long or Short

Difficulty: 8

The Big W makes me a lot of money. It's simple and powerful and very few people use it; which is why it probably works.

If you think about fundamental patterns the basic 'down up' move is a V. Down then up. The next level of complexity is a W: down, up, down, up.

A W move can, therefore, be thought of as a fall with recovery with a hesitation at the bottom.

With any large fall you can imagine a little hesitation is often in order.

Now I will have to detour into some maths and I will upset math-heads once again by waving my hands about and being grossly general.

Markets are fractal. There is a bucket of implications to this but one is they are self-affine.

This means if you have little Ws in the chart, you're going to get a big one at a larger scale.

You can now be happy in the knowledge that hundreds of math people now have white foam pouring from their mouths from reading this.

The upshot is, especially in a crash, look for the last leg of the W before jumping in.

While mathematicians are chewing on their belt you can skip onto the internet and take a look at the Dow for the last 20 years (available on ADVFN) and count the Ws at the bottoms of corrections and crashes and the next time the market goes off a cliff as you sense the hesitation before the recovery, you can watch a new W form and wait until the last leg to go long.

Meanwhile, as an aside, the bottoms of the W also give a nice steer on the Bullish or Bearishness of the long-term trend. A higher second U is Bullish and a lower one Bearish. It's kind of obvious.

The thing to remember is, these patterns form on the basis of millions of people getting up to speed with what is going on in the world around us. Some are slower or more cautious than others, so waves of information take time to percolate into the price and the bigger the change the longer it takes.

However, no indicator can predict the unknowable, so if the extinction comet heads towards Earth, the market will not react until after the five minutes it takes for the operator of the Hubble telescope to call his broker has elapsed.

(chart overleaf)

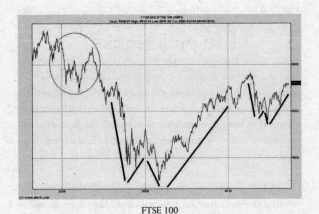

FTSE 100

Answers begin with W too.

Common sense ways to pick stocks

Common sense is a misnomer. We all know common sense is just not that common. The markets are full of sharks out after your money. If you want to test that hypothesis, take £10,000, split it into ten lots of £1000 then ask ten random advisers what to do with a thousand pounds. Do it and then come back in a year and see what you have left.

Well actually let's not do that, as we know it will be an expensive lesson.

My point is 'bullshit baffles brains' in the market, when in reality common sense is a great way to make money. However, common sense, apart from being rare, is not the ritzy story people want to hear when they invest their money. They buy the sizzle not the steak. Lots of clever mumbo-jumbo sells. Nevertheless, it is unlikely to make you money.

On the other hand common sense does. The trouble with common sense is it is boring and involves work. However, people who think making money can be done without effort and hard work will be disappointed.

You can swim the seas with the big fish because as a small investor you fit a niche which the market pays you to fill. However, you still have to swim hard and keep your wits about you.

Know your company

Signal: Long or Short

Difficulty: 5

You can definitely invest in a company and know bugger all about what it does. Many investors will be quite smug in this fact. This is because in a Bull market even a chimp throwing poo at the FT to make its share selections will make money. Nevertheless, it can't hurt to know what the company you are investing in does.

You can actually know a company better than the City if you so chose. How many highly paid fund managers go into a cheap furniture enterprise or drop in to drink at the out of town locations of a pub chain?

You might actually do business with a company and know whether its business is booming or slumping. You are assured to have a much better view on the company than any Oxford grad climbing the slippery pole in some brokerage in the Square Mile.

A chartist will say everyone's opinions are already in the share's chart, so you don't need to know if the CEO is bonkers or a genius, or whether its business is suddenly booming or not, because the market knows all.

This could be right, it may well be right for a BP or Vodafone company, but outside of the top 500 companies, the City is pretty much lost for a clear view of what is going on. The City will tell you with a curl of the lip that anything under £500,000,000 in value is a small company.

This is great news, because while they go off to lunch you can get to know these small companies in detail and get to spot the ones about to rise above the myopic radar of the City.

Remember: the market pays you to make it efficient. Getting to know companies, particularly smaller ones is a place it will pay you to help it.

Know your company's product

Signal: Long or Short

Difficulty: 5

Apple used to be a lame duck. Microsoft practically had to rescue it by taking a pile of shares to keep it afloat. Now it's the second most valuable company in the whole of the USA. What happened?

iPod, iPhone, iPad.

Three products = $200 billion in valuation.

This could be a very short section because being the common sense section this should set you on the right track.

Product releases, especially for small companies, can be make or break events and you can often cut through all the rhubarb released by a company and its brokers just by studying its product.

It's a simple thing, but does it have a price list? You would be amazed at the companies that do not. Do you want to own shares in that company?

Does the product exist? Is it out yet? When can you take delivery?

Is it any good?

I once had dealings with a drug company which had an amazing product for the aging amongst us. For some reason the MD, who was not a spring lamb, didn't take it. It was packaged very poorly. Did that make me want to buy its shares? No it did not.

It is hard for a good company to have bad products, so if you want to invest in good companies for the long-term, check out the product. It will give you a lead on the professionals.

Get to know the company's industry

Signal: Long or Short

Difficulty: 5

A good place to start is the industry you are in. You are a legal insider. That is to say you know more about the industry and the companies in the industry than any City slicker; you know how it works, you know its dirty secrets, you know the personalities, the gossip and what's more your knowledge is legal to use because it's in the public domain. Your edge is you are steeped in the industry, whereas the City has only a handful of overpaid Uni grads to look in on the whole bewildering mess.

Again the market will pay for your expertise to improve the efficiency of the market.

Of course your industry might be slow and you won't get rich over night. Nevertheless, over time it will do you well and what is better it's a good place to start your investing career. For one thing you'll most likely avoid the dogs.

One thing to be careful of, however, is over investing; particularly if you are actually employed by a company you buy stock in. Remember: diversification is a law to be broken at your peril.

Read the specialist press

As you may have picked up from the previous points, the City is not necessarily populated by the smartest folk. It is a privileged world where selling is often more important than doing. As such there are a lot of slick talkers to be found and not as many smart technicians as you'd imagine. This means that important information that will affect share prices is often quite slow to penetrate the workings of the market and thus information can take a long time to percolate to the City.

It's the same in the mainstream news. What appears in an academic journal can take six months to show up in a magazine like the New Scientist or the Economist and take another six months to appear in the national press. That's a full year before the news actually gets to the mainstream listener.

As an investor you want to be reading the academic journal.

However, there aren't any academic journals for most industries. The equivalent is specialist press. There is a magazine for almost every specialist subject and industry. I'm sure somewhere there is a Toffee Makers Monthly! (I Googled it and there isn't.) Whatever is the latest thing in the toffee industry will be in the magazine months before the City knows about it. As such, if you are following a company closely or a sector (or two) keenly, getting the trade press will give you a leap on the City and an investment edge.

Again the market is paying you to improve its efficiency. If you know a lot about a company you invest in, the products it has and their competition and you are following the industry and its press, it is common sense you'll be in a small group of expert investors and therefore likely to do better than most.

Once you are, you will find there aren't many people out there like you. This is why you'll excel.

Call up the FD and say 'Hello.'

Signal: Long or Short

Difficulty: 7

This is hard because most people are intimidated by someone with a grand title like FD or CFO. However, rest assured the FD of a PLC puts his underpants on one leg at a time like everyone else.

Frankly if he won't take your call, especially if it's the CFO of a small company, it's a bad sign in itself. The FD is not a busy man, or rather if he is he must be having trouble. He may not want to talk to you; that's another matter. If he doesn't want to talk to you, you shouldn't buy his stock.

There are no paparazzi outside his front door and if he's any good at his job he'll have time on his hands. He is just like you, he answers calls he wants and doesn't answer calls he doesn't want to take.

If he doesn't want to take a quick shareholder's call, there is a problem with the business.

If he takes your call, that's a thumbs up immediately. If he's on holiday, that's a bad sign. Some company directors seem to be constantly on holiday; this shouldn't fill you with confidence.

OK, so the FD of Vodafone may be busy but most small

company CFOs should be reachable. When you get through, ask a few questions and gauge whether you'd buy a used car from him. If you would, then that's a fair sign the company is in good hands.

Now you could apply this rule to the CEO. He is the top guy after all. However, don't waste your breath. The CEO is likely to be a first-class salesman. He could sell you London Bridge if he wanted to. CEOs get to the top job by charming the birds out of the trees. You will likely fall under the spell as much as anyone else.

The FD, on the other hand, is a number crunching nerd. He can sell you a pup with numbers, but magic with words is not his strong suit.

What is hot in the States

Signal: Long

Difficulty: 4

In classic efficient market hypothesis, information travels instantaneously and prices jump to hit their correct level immediately. You can see this at work when news appears. The price spikes almost immediately and rises in seconds to a new level of balance. However, watch the market long enough and you will see lags. Sometimes the lags last seconds, sometimes minutes and sometimes hours. Earlier in the book I suggested that market symmetries mean things are similar over different scales. As such, lags can also be weeks, months and years. A good example can fall to common sense. What's hot in the US today will be hot in the UK tomorrow.

A prime example of this was the dotcom bubble. The US Nasdaq market had been fizzing for two years with IPOs like Netscape before the UK market experienced the beginning of the frenzy. I know because I was a director of one of the first UK companies (Online PLC) that went into orbit when the bubble hit the UK. I had watched rather desolately as Silicon Valley companies exploded into overnight successes while Online languished, then suddenly the penny dropped in the UK and Online's share price exploded 1000%.

What was big in the US finally made it across the pond.

This has happened for decades. The US originates the big

idea and at some point it gets to the UK. Now it doesn't take too much effort to watch US trends and, once you do, you will see tomorrow happening today in the US. Then you add that to your investment ideas and await your opportunity.

Right now 'fraking' is big news in the US... It's just a matter of time before it's big news in Europe. Meanwhile you can figure out now how to get in on the ground floor.

Way 32

What is hot in Japan

Signal: Long

Difficulty: 4

This should be a very short entry. Japan has, over the last decade or so, also reached a level of economic and cultural maturity and dominance to set the big trends. When little girls start wearing strange footwear or playing with weird electronics: take note.

Right now Japan is into robotics. Remember that, because in five years it will be big here.

The US tends to lead by one to two years but Japan tends to be further ahead. This is because the Japanese can have a rather non-commercial streak, which is rather British in a Victorian kind of way. This means they set pre-commercial trends. At some point they go commercial. Robot football is not going to be big soon, but robots will be big someday and when they are they will be very big indeed.

I could make Way 33: What is hot in China, but that is yet to come. Bear it in mind, because investing is a long-term game and the rules evolve.

The market has crystal balls

Signal: Long or Short

Difficulty: 5

When you pick a stock don't look to the news today. Today is gone and the market is looking much further ahead than that. This is why good results do not make the price rise. The market is expecting the result so it's no big deal. The market is looking one year out.

That is to say it is factoring in everything it can guess about for the next 12 months or so. This is because most investors have a one year horizon for their investments.

As such, you need to think about where a company will be 18 months to two years out. This sounds hard but actually it's quite easy. Right now the nationalised UK banks Lloyds and RBS are struggling along, they look like they are at a 50% discount to similar banks. That makes sense; they have a lot of healing to do.

Is this gap going to shrink in six months? Who knows?

In three years?

Well that seems highly likely. So even if it only closed half the gap in three years, you'd still be looking good with a 50% profit.

In the market, short-term horizons make for uncertainty; long-term horizons are much more predictable. The trouble is most people hate the idea of getting rich slowly. That is a big mistake.

So when the market is filled with doom-laden news and there has just been a crash, don't be surprised if the market is rising; it's looking one to two years ahead and so should you.

Taxi ads

Signal: Short

Difficulty: 4

Unlike publicity, all advertising is not good advertising. Taxi ads are as bad an investment omen as you can get.

For some reason companies doomed to failure love to advertise on and in taxis. It's not a particularly expensive way of advertising, at least in terms of the size of the cheque you have to write. Nonetheless, taxis seem to carry publicity for companies doomed to go down the pan.

This may be because companies with a lot of money to spend on a make or break launch end up shovelling it indiscriminately in all directions in an orgy of desperate spending. The taxi livery and seat ads are a final resort in this carpet bombing approach.

As a money Yoda might say: Throwing money around, a successful company does not make.

It's not the taxi's fault, as such, it's just that any company that is so desperate to push itself forwards with advertising, is probably in the process of throwing so much money out of the window that it will soon go broke.

Of the army of dotcom busts, few seemed able to resist the taxi and even today, the new brands come and go, never to return.

Keep your eye out for phone box advertising too; also a good signal for a short.

The curse of the shirt deal

Signal: Short

Difficulty: 5

A company taking ads on taxis is a bad sign, but at least, in the common sense stakes, you can see how an advert driving around London costing little money could be a good selling proposition.

Yet on first blush, from a common sense point of view, how can it make sense to pay millions of pounds to have your name on a football shirt?

Undoubtedly a great salesman could present to me and you and dazzle us with science and have the ignorant scales fall from our eyes to see in full Technicolor why it makes perfect sense to blow a fortune on having your company name on a bunch of youngsters kicking a football. I'm sure we wouldn't be swayed by the bragging rights of a big bunch of tickets to all the games; for friends and family and customers with an amazing box with incredible views, I'm sure the reasons will be strictly commercial. Isn't the whole country transfixed by football?

However, many companies doing these kinds of deal, and doing them big, have gone spectacularly bust.

AIG was on Manchester United's shirt, Northern Rock on Newcastle United's. Man City and Accident Group,

Charlton and AllSports, West Ham and the XL airline; all these companies came horribly unglued.

Perhaps a company doing a shirt deal is actually just out of control.

You can extend this idea to companies that put their names on stadiums and to firms that sponsor Formula One.

Remember the Enron Stadium and the Parmalat Formula One team?

This of course could be what is known as observer bias, in so much as you don't notice companies that do these deals and don't go bust.

Yet even so, the thought is, why would you throw such titanic money around on these kind of unaccountable deals which have no measurable returns if you were running a smart business? Manchester United is a great team, but $100 million to put your logo on 11 shirts is surely a sign of a kind of unexpressed insanity. It's easy to come up with a lot of bad reasons to do so but not many good ones.

As such, when you're thinking of selecting a stock or shorting one, this kind of trophy marketing is a red flag.

Buy to the sound of cannons

Signal: Long

Difficulty: 6

Apparently Rothschild coined this phrase and as a big fan of his wine I have to go along with him. It doesn't really make sense that the market should have a big rally when a war kicks off but it seems to happen.

The last instance of this was in 2004 when the Iraq War Version Two kicked off. That was the spark of the recovery post dotcom. It was a rally that made lots of people rich and didn't end until the credit crunch snuffed it out.

One of the reasons a war can spark a rally is it removes uncertainty. Whereas no one knew how far up the creek everyone was on the run up to war and were consequentially selling, the outbreak of war clears the fog and replaces fear with excitement.

Excitement may not be stupid, as countries throw large quantities of money around in wars and people in the right place get to shovel it up. Therefore a war can be a reflationary period and while there is great misery somewhere, there are lots of people with extra cash about the economy making the tills ring.

Of course defence businesses will do well and there are obvious choices to be made with a war on the go, but buying to the sound of cannons may simply mean buying stocks on your 'probable' investment list or putting your cash reserves into already established investments to take advantage of a rally.

We obviously hope there won't be an opportunity to put this idea into practice, but if and when that sad day comes again it makes sense to let the market pay you to help it out by being an optimist.

Of course in a really big nasty war like WW2 it made perfect sense to go 'all in' when you got off the boat from Dunkirk. Shares were unsurprisingly low at that point. However, if we had lost the pound would have been worthless anyway, as such buying was a one way bet.

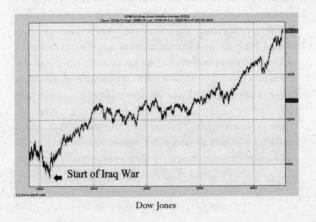

Dow Jones

Sad but true: war is good business.

Accounting irregularity

Signal: Short

Difficulty: 5

There are really few reasons to sell stocks you like. Clearly you can want to sell because you have done well and are happy to reinvest the gains in companies with more upside. However, reasons to simply cut and run are few. These are the same kinds of reasons to short, so the reason for a Bull to bail is a reason for a Bear to pounce.

A clear signal to bail is an accounting irregularity. Companies that can't get their books straight are not to be trusted. You should not buy companies that can't keep track of their assets. There are very few harmless reasons for accountancy irregularities and an infinite number of toxic ones. As such you should expect the worst if you hear a company discovering one. It is often a prelude to complete collapse.

Either way, a company that can't control its bookkeeping is unlikely to be able to control its business model. As such, a company with accounting irregularities is probably doomed.

Death of a salesman

Signal: Short

Difficulty: 5

It's morbid but it remains a phenomenon that the death of the CEO of a high flying company can bring about the company's collapse.

This is because the company may be, in effect, a one man band, whose future depends on the intricate knowledge of the industry, customers and internal status of the company that only the CEO can master. It can also be that the CEO is the kind of financial juggler who alone can keep the rocket ship on course. This is a polite way of explaining why, for example, Robert Maxwell's empire imploded within weeks of his death.

How many companies could have imploded in the credit crunch had the senior management not been there to fight a rearguard action on the brink of a corporate abyss?

When tragedy strikes, if you hold or are looking to short companies then you should pay close attention to the replacement or demise of a high flying company, high flying management.

We have covered 'up like a rocket and down like a stick' earlier and this is another example.

Sometimes it doesn't even take the death of a CEO, merely his replacement, to trigger implosion. If the new management hits a situation they don't understand or can't manage, they are very capable of pulling the plug on a company rather than stepping aside.

Now, if that high flying company had a penchant for football shirt deals and had just suffered an accounting irregularity you wouldn't even need to look at those stock charts to make a quick decision.

Portfolio: diversify or die

Signal: Long or Short

Difficulty: 5

You must have a portfolio if you want to survive investing in the market. Do not listen to anybody, not even Warren Buffett, who tells you not to. If you do not have a portfolio the chances are you will lose your shirt.

Do not put all your eggs in one basket. We all understand that. This is the law of having a portfolio.

I believe 30 plus stocks is the target to aim for. Now you will say, 'I only have enough money for three stocks'.

That is OK; buy three and then save towards four. If you double your money on one stock and sell, go on to buy two new stocks, not one.

You will get to 30 stocks in the end, probably quite fast. Then you can buy more of each new stock, but not before.

30 stocks will mean your portfolio's performance will start to look like the FTSE 100, but if you pick well it will go up more and go down less. The point is avoid the sort of wealth-crashing SNAFU that you would have suffered if you'd had four tech stocks in the dotcom crash or all your money in Northern Rock in 2007.

The more risk you want to take, the bigger your portfolio has to be. If you want to buy small crazy stocks you might need to get to 40 before you are safe from getting squished by a run of bad luck.

Diversify should mean spreading yourself over sectors too. There is no point holding 30 different gold mines; you won't be diversified outside of mining. What you need to do is build your tool bag of investing rules then apply these to a broad range of companies across a broad range of sectors. Why not go further and think about being diversified across the global markets?

Diversity is strength.

Classically you should buy a load of stocks, a bag of bonds and keep say 10% in cash. However we aren't looking at bonds and cash in this book, we are picking stocks, so you can go down that route too, if you please, while still building a stock portfolio under that umbrella.

Investors that don't want to build a diversified portfolio using this book may as well throw it in the bin now. After they have lost their shirt, maybe they can buy another copy and start again from scratch. Many investors have to spend a lot of money to learn this lesson. Don't be one of them.

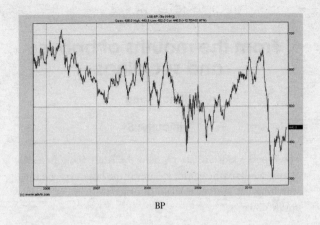

BP

Just one more reason why you wouldn't put all your money in a single company, even if it was a very long established super blue chip.

From the mouths of babes and sucklings

Signal: Long

Difficulty: 5

Those pesky kids are always onto the latest thing first. As mature adults of the world, we are far too busy to spend time searching out the latest trend in order to turn our worlds upside down.

There are still a couple of older generations that haven't got to grips with computers and maybe never will. How were they to know that they should have bought Google or Apple stock?

If they had stalked their grandchildren they might have seen it coming.

Stupid things that kids do often turn out to be the smart things middle-aged people can't get their heads around.

Keeping an eye on what kids are up to is an opportunity to get in early because kids don't buy shares and the oldies in the City, who have all the money, don't do new.

At some point even the grey-haired get the picture and suddenly off goes the price of the stock making the stuff that the kids have been loving for a couple of years.

This might sound implausible, but anyone buying Games Workshop when it got the rights to the *Lord of the Rings* film license, will attest that while little metal figures pushed around a board based on a '60s book loved by hippies, might sound quaint, it was also something that rocketed the price of the company by multiples.

Now if you had read the trade press, known the product and watched the kids practically living in Games Workshop stores, you would have made a pretty penny.

Not for sale

Signal: Long

Difficulty: 7

Every now and again you will come across a share you can't buy. It may sound perverse, but some shares can't be had in enough volume to be worthwhile.

Back in the pit of the credit crunch I decided to buy some Pendragon, a car dealer. I only wanted a little because the stock looked set to go bust as it had fallen well over 90% of its pre-crash and was in the car selling business. It was therefore dependant on credit and selling cars; two bad places to be at the end of a financial crash.

However, even though I only wanted a couple of thousand pounds of stock, there was none to be had. My broker scoured all the market makers and gave the market makers' cages a good rattling but he simply could not find the stock. In the end, after three days, a small bag of stock was found and I added it to my portfolio. Once the market started to recover it shot up 1000%.

Supply and demand is meant to drive the market and it does in normal times and for normal stocks, but when you get into the less mainstream places or trade the more outlandish times, this rule stops applying. As such if you find a beaten down share which you can't buy a sensible quantity of, it's likely to be a good long-term buy.

Only an idiot would give up trying to buy a cheap stock no one wants to sell. Right now I've been trying to buy one listed stock on AIM for four months. It is an oddball but if I do get some, I will be happy in the knowledge that if anything good happens to the company, its share price will explode in value. Am I going to say which stock it is? NO!

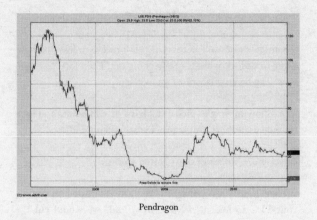

Pendragon

Ironically it can be hard to buy at the bottom.

Making an offer that can't be refused

Signal: Long or Short

Difficulty: 7

Common sense isn't necessarily easy to use unless you have a key to unlock what is really going on. Therefore common sense can be an offshoot of knowledge.

The following way to pick a stock is a case in point. You have to understand this simple process and 'Private Equity.'

This is how 'Private Equity' often works:

Private Equity to manager: 'We are interested in buying your PLC to take it private. If we did, we would cut the management into 20% of the shares of the business.'

Manager to Private Equity: 'That is mighty fine of you because I currently own 0.001% of the company's shares.'

Private Equity to manager: 'The trouble is your share price is too high for us to buy this public company, but we will be happy to talk when the share price is much lower and we can all make a huge profit from the deal.'

Manager to Private Equity: 'Let's talk next year then.'

Of course this should be a crime, but it isn't. Not surprisingly this has happened a lot over the years.

So as an investor you look for a good business with a good set of books but a very depressed management.

Even though the business seems to be piling up cash, even though sales are healthy, the management is accentuating the negative at every turn. Of course the share price keeps falling. At some point the price will stop falling and there will be a lull. Then, voila, up will pop a private equity bid. Of course the management will then complain that the market didn't understand the company and recommend the offer, which will generally be at a 40% premium to the lull in the price fall.

Now if you have seen your stock fall from 400p to 100p, 140p a share seems like a rescue, especially if you are a pension fund that has so much stock it can't get out of the company's stock without driving it further off a cliff.

As an investor that bought around 100p you feel great too. All you did was use your common sense to see that the figures didn't match the manager's presentation of the state of the company, to look at the chart to see the long share price swoon was over and bore in mind Private Equity loves a cheap deal.

With this little insight into 'Private Equity' everything makes perfect sense, both on the way down and on the way up to takeover.

Invest in the obvious

Signal: Long

Difficulty: 6

Investment managers like to call them themes. We would probably call themes: 'obvious things happening around us'.

Young people can't stop using their phones. China will get more important. People will live longer and longer. Flu will one day soon kill lots of people…and so on.

Once you feel something is obvious, you should back it in your portfolio.

If you think that one day soon classic antibiotics will stop working, you would search out companies researching new ones. If it is obvious to you that the world will go hungry, you will look to buy a fertiliser company or two.

We all see a few obvious things that are bound to happen, yet most people won't see your insights and often will violently disagree with them. What is blindingly obvious to you will be opaque to most and likewise their insights will be incomprehensible to you. Being right is not a democratic process and no one, except me and you of course, has a monopoly on it.

Broadcasting with my ADVFN hat on, I called the crash for nearly 18 months before the balloon went up and right up until it all came tumbling down, people looked at me as if I'd been released from the funny farm. When I called the bottom people thought I was crazy too.

The lesson is, always back what you think is obvious to you, especially if others miss the point. You do not have to be a brilliant guy or have an opinion on every subject, just one, now and again, will do nicely.

Listen to our lords and masters

Signal: Long

Difficulty: 6

Business people think they are tough and smart, which is why they are often tempted into politics. However, they are slouches compared to politicians and often get eaten alive in the realm of politics and government. This is why you should never back business against government. Government will always win. Politicians wipe out whole industries, lock people in jail, go to war etc; business is just a pussy cat in comparison, a convenient 'milch cow' with no real power against government when push comes to shove.

This is why you should listen to government and trade their position. What they say ultimately goes.

Government is also slow to react so, if you can define the political course set upon, you can trade it for a long time and let it build.

This goes for all investments from Forex right down to small companies. The leviathan of government sets the agenda for a country's economy; it is one of those big pictures.

If government is green, buy into wind farms. If it is blue, sell stocks that service councils. If it is red invest in nursing homes and bridge builders.

It's not that difficult.

Takeovers

Signal: Long

Difficulty: 8

Everyone loves a takeover and in normal circumstances takeovers are rife. This is not because they are good for shareholders per se, but because the City and managers make big pay days when they happen. If you run a business well, you have plenty of time for strategy and plenty of money at your disposal to play such games as empire building.

Research shows that takeovers destroy value, but let's not allow facts to ruin a fun game.

As investors we love them; it's like the finale to a good film.

The obvious way to find a takeover target, apart from looking for management trying to sell out their shareholders, is to look for industries 'ripe for consolidation.' Ripe for consolidation is City speak for 'unable to resist being plundered.'

This might be because an industry has borrowed a mountain of debt and is therefore reliant on its bankers for money.

At this point an industry has to take note of its banker's advice to buy X and sell Y and merge with A or take over B. Of course the bankers are doing it for the best, not the mind bending fees they will earn.

Nonetheless, this event won't happen overnight. You have plenty of time to join the party.

There will be plenty of sage writing about strategy. If businesses are vertical, they will need to broaden out. If they are broad they will need to focus on their core business by selling off un-strategic businesses and so on.

This talk will give you plenty of time to jump on board a trend. Normally small companies get bought by big ones, so that if a market is going to consolidate, you need only size the players up to see who is going to be buying and who is going to get sold.

You want to buy the company getting gobbled up.

The gathering interest and excitement will push up the whole sector. As such, it's a win win scenario. You don't even have to get it right to do well, you just buy a good looking company using your other picking tricks and add an extra bit of zip by picking a company in the crosshairs of a takeover scenario.

But you want a hard tip. Always buy a company where a director that buys is an old retired politician. This old chap usually needs a very good reason to buy and a very close horizon to sell and you can be sure that they've got plenty of paperwork to prove the fact they were clear to trade. When a takeover comes the old politico will be out on his ear and, now long forgotten, headed for the scrap heap. When he buys, follow him.

Takeovers: selling the buyers

Signal: Short

Difficulty: 8

Some people just aren't happy to make money going long, so even when it comes to takeovers they want to make money going short.

It is common sense that the party writing the big cheque is going to get a fat bill and end up with a big bag of problems to sort out. This won't be good news for the company in the short-term.

If you were a hedge fund manager you would buy the company getting bought and sell the company buying.

The company getting bought will be at a discount to the offer because something could go wrong and there is also a wait involved, meanwhile the heavy lifting of the buying company will squeeze its price down.

You can take advantage of this.

Nevertheless, if a company is on a buying spree it can end up bending the company out of shape. The key is to watch an acquiring company go off·on a binge and then once it has bloated itself, short it.

It will be up to its ears in debt, drowning in dysfunctional acquisitions and exhausted for funds. This is a good time for ghoulish investors to come out and kick the company as the market is sure to.

Know the long-term

Signal: Long

Difficulty: 7

Timing the market in the short-term is extremely difficult. 'Extremely difficult' means, in investor language, impossible. So why try and pull it off?

Instead know the long-term.

In the long-term the UK has a shortage of electricity generation. I know this but not many people seem to. Don't ask me why.

However, why would I not own DRAX? (A big power station in the Midlands). Well it burns coal for one. Oh dear.

I can see how that pans out when the lights of Birmingham and Manchester start to flicker. No one is going to be thinking about polar bears drowning then. What's more, it's a cheap company paying a fat dividend right now. Knowing simple things a few years out puts a very simple complexion on them.

People do not think long-term and do not invest for it. That makes this tack very lucrative and kind of easy. It's like inhabiting an empty land full of fertile fields. Meanwhile everyone is fighting over tomorrow and next month and next quarter; fighting over scraps.

Of course you want to get rich quick, but getting rich slow is much easier because no one is trying to do that.

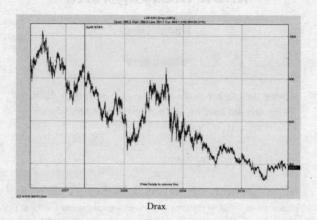

Drax

Doesn't anyone know the UK will be short of electricity in a few years time?

Know your risk

Signal: Long

Difficulty: 7

Risk is badly understood; in fact it may even be a misnomer. Some people would call buying a crazy small cap stock, run from a faraway place by people whose names can't be Googled, high risk. I wouldn't. There is practically no risk, you are almost certain to lose your money.

It is important to know the risks you are taking and to look for what might bite you. The credit crunch was caused because 99% of people in the financial markets didn't know where the risk was. They thought there wasn't any.

The risk they thought they had removed had just been scraped up into a giant pile and stuffed in a basement somewhere. When it finally escaped we all know what happened.

If you have a handle on the risk you are taking you can manage it and use it to make you more money, but the amount of risk doesn't come written down on a label, you just have to work it out. A good place to start is to imagine it is a lot higher risk than you might have guessed.

Another recommended way of getting your judgement of risk right is not to believe a word of what any party tells you. Pretend you are Sherlock Holmes at a murder and try to piece together the 'real story.'

Try to understand why the price is where it is, then you can counter that with your arguments.

Beaten up brands

Signal: Long

Difficulty: 5

In this age of celebrity and branding it's hard to imagine that brands can be undervalued. However they can be, and when they are an investor should look at the share very closely. Quite often the brand is unvalued in the share price, sometimes you could be forgiven for thinking is was a liability.

Food companies often have good brands and this sector is a good example of one where companies and brands can get beaten down. Brands always have a better ability to make a comeback because quite often fashions come and go and stocks with brands can oscillate accordingly.

The brand can be utterly out of fashion too and perhaps even obsolete but stocking an old brand on an updated idea can suddenly bring a company back to life or simply save it from the dustbin.

The following is the stock chart of Hornby, makers of model trains and slot cars. New management, old brand and some news ideas can be a potent combination.

(chart overleaf)

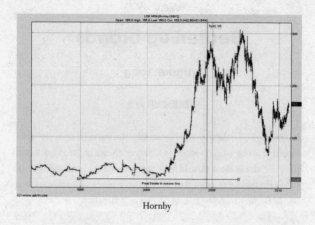

Hornby

Hornby is still making Scalextrics and model railways...apparently the City didn't like it a few years ago, but fashion turned.

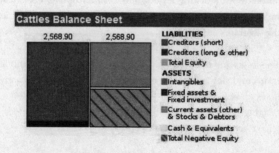

Negative Equity

Signal: Short

Difficulty: 4

Technically this is quite a difficult idea to understand, but it is easy to spot.

Opposite page bottom left, is a graphic from ADVFN of a company with negative equity. See the stripy chunk in assets? That's the amount of negative equity.

What is it? Negative Equity is the same for shareholders and for home owners. Negative Equity is when the amount you owe is more than the asset you own is worth.

If you borrow £300,000 on a house and it's now worth £290,000, the negative equity is £10,000. As a home owner, you are £10,000 in the hole.

Companies can be the same. They owe more than all their assets. In a world without credit, it's called bust, but in the world of corporate bonds and credit, it is called highly geared.

Avoid these companies and if you find one and it hasn't fallen a long way you might think of shorting it.

Companies get this way because our friends 'Private Equity' buy companies with assets, then strip those assets out and pay themselves with them. The company then borrows a ton of money and the Private Equity people sell the company back onto the market; normally to our pension funds. These institutions are not bright enough to care they are buying a business back they only recently sold from the people they sold it to a couple of years back. Except now the company has had its assets plundered and is in a world of debt but for some reason is worth much more. It's one of the more obviously legal crimes in the City: you couldn't make it up.

The reason the companies can exist at all in this state is they make enough cash to pay down the loans from the profits they make and can keep the banks off their backs. If things get tricky, they go back to their new owners and ask for more capital via a rights issue to replace the cash recently stripped. It would be funny if your pension wasn't footing the bill.

In theory if a company like this gets beaten down to the lowly value it's really worth, it could be a good buy when and if good times roll. This is because coming back from the brink can do wonders for a share price. A booming period will help a company pay off its loans and get healthy again. Apparently this is an efficient capital structure.

However, as I write, we are in the middle of a nasty recession so that's not currently an investment option. However, this idea is worth bearing in mind for 2013-2014*, when the economy will start to sizzle again, yet there are probably many better places to look.

*Market timing is impossible so please exchange these dates for the words 'sometime in the future.'

Golden rule No. 4

A pinch of salt required

When it comes to investing, don't believe anything as gospel. Don't believe the newspapers, the management, the friend with a tip or your own ability to get it right. Everything at best is probable and anything is possible. Management is over optimistic, brokers are flaky, facts are malleable and your insight patchy.

If you keep this jaundice perspective you won't go far wrong because one thing is for sure, there are plenty of bad people out to part you from your money.

Tracker funds: simple exposure

Research into stock picking suggests that you can't beat the market; you can only jump on board. Clearly it's hard to jump on the whole FTSE 100 because buying 100 shares in the right proportion is difficult, expensive and complicated. However, the idea was taken up by financial companies who created tradable shares that replicated the FTSE 100 or the Dow. These are called tracker funds or ETFs. ETF stands for Exchange Traded Fund and gives investors and traders a way of getting exposure to things like gold or indexes inside their share portfolios. Ways 51-52 use ETFs.

Exchange Traded Funds. Buy a FTSE tracker

Signal: Long

Difficulty: 1

An index tracker is a share made by a financial company that follows an index as it moves. If the FTSE goes up 10%, a FTSE tracker goes up 10%.

Let's say you don't want to go ferreting around the market picking stocks, but you think the stock market will go up. In this case you would just buy the FTSE 100 tracker and sit back. The famous UK one is the iShares FTSE 100 ETF (ADVFN:ISF)

You pay one brokerage commission and you get a profit or loss depending on exactly what the FTSE 100 does. It's that simple and it's supersonically cheap.

With a FTSE tracker, you can throw your arms in the air and say, 'I don't care about the details but over the next 30 years shares are going up big and I'm buying £1000 of FTSE tracker every three months forever and this is my equity strategy.' It isn't such a bad idea either. Books have been written to explain why this is the only way to go and to disagree is to challenge some Nobel prize-winning economists to calculus at dawn.

Of course no broker or bank is going to get fat on that, no

fund or fund of funds or hedge fund manager is going to drive a Porsche 911 down Threadneedle Street looking cool, if that lesson was taught to all eleven years olds at school. So it's hardly surprising no one is taking big adverts out saying, why not do it the easy way; buy a FTSE tracker and forget about making us fat and happy. Hell, if you listened to that kind of talk you'd never buy this book, so please don't pass this tip on.

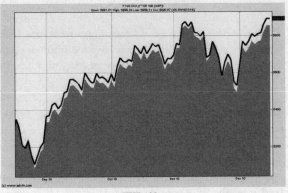

FTSE 100

This is a chart of the FTSE 100 (in black) trading alongside the FTSE 100 tracker (in grey).

Commodity ETFs. You really want to buy commodities, you really, really want to?

Signal: Long

Difficulty: 8

There is nothing like a good benign investment idea with little room for error to attract someone to twist the idea into something almost guaranteed to blow your face off.

ETF index trackers have bred all sorts of trackers of a very dubious nature. The whole idea is to wrap up a diversified portfolio into a single stock for cheap, cost effective, efficient tracking of a broad market index. Now companies are coming up with leveraged ETFs on all sorts of obscure and non-broad instruments and in many cases they don't even track properly.

For example a commodity ETF, say wheat, gives you exposure in a share to wheat prices.

Now for some reason if you wanted to put wheat or gold in your share portfolio you could buy a commodity ETF and, lo and behold, you would have it.

Now you might have an extremely good reason to have wheat in your share portfolio, so it is not an utterly silly idea, but you should rest assured you need to have an extremely good reason in mind to do so. Commodities are a great way of making a small fortune from a large one.

However, if you are a farmer and locusts have just shown up, you might be onto something, but if you are in a town reading a newspaper warning about food security, you can rest assured that it's already in the price and you are investing blind.

Let the computer do the work

You may know the sort of company you fancy buying. Let's say you want a big company with a fat dividend but a low P/E. The trouble is you don't want to go over all two thousand companies in the UK, line by line. A share screener like ADVFN's FilterX lets you put in your criteria and pluck out all the companies that fit the bill. Ways 53-60 are some interesting areas to apply those filters to.

P/E, the basic cheap or not cheap indicator

Signal: Short

Difficulty: 4

P/E means price earnings ratio. It is, in effect, the number of year's profit it takes to buy the company for its current market value. Crudely, a 10 P/E means the same as a company worth £10m making a £1m profit.

P/Es can be all over the shop. A loss-making company really doesn't have one although the Americans say it has a negative P/E. Likewise, a company that makes a few thousand in a year yet is worth many millions might have a P/E of 20,000.

So, at the margins, P/E can get a little useless. However, over say three or four and less than 100 P/E means a lot.

As an investor who wants to buy a cheap company, a P/E under 12 and above say four, will interest you.

If you were going searching for cheap companies, throwing away all companies outside this range is a good place to start.

P/E is not the whole story but it is certainly an attractive attribute. Good companies with low P/Es make good investments.

Sales have value—high sales to market capitalisation

Signal: Short

Difficulty: 4

Many will disagree, but having spent my entire life building businesses I can assure you, selling product is tough. Like most things you can achieve big sales buying selling to cheap or shipping commodities at cost. There are always ways of cheating. However, a for a sensible business, selling a lot of normal stuff is not an easy matter.

As such, a sensible company with a low company valuation that sells a lot of its product, could well be cheap.

A drugs company can be worth £100 million selling £15 million of drugs. This is sales, not profits. This gives it a 4x ratio of market capitalisation to sales; meanwhile some companies can be worth only 10% of the sales. Can a drug company's £1 of sales really be worth 40 times one of these companies' lowly enterprises? To me the answer is unlikely.

In extreme situations some companies could be bought by the cash flow created by extending their credit terms by three weeks. It is no wonder that it is not unknown for a large company with a 10% of sales valuation to get bought by an entrepreneur, then ask its suppliers for a 5% discount of current invoices. This can be half the cost of buying the company!

So a company with big sales but a lowly valuation is an interesting candidate. Squeezing a couple of percentage points out of the business process could make a huge difference to the business.

Not many people look at this number but it works time and again for me. In the end, 'talk is cheap' but 'money talks'.

Get over techno-fear. Let the robot sort you out

Signal: Long

Difficulty: 6

Once you have a few, or for that matter many, financial criteria, you can put them into a 'screener' or 'scanner.' ADVFN's is called FilterX. The FilterX screener will chop out companies that don't fit your bill and prune down the 2000+ stocks to a handful. This select group can then be further interrogated by looking at charts and news, or whatever tool you fancy, to qualify or otherwise the next stock to go into your portfolio.

This is a very efficient way to get a list of candidates onto your radar. Only when you have a refined universe of companies can you stake them out and watch their stories develop. That way you can get to know likely companies and get a feel for how their story is progressing.

You can play about with the parameters and move them around to see who almost fits, or tune in to different groups using different values.

Believe it or not, chopping out chunks of the market and seeing who fits the bill can be amusing. It also builds up your market knowledge.

The whole stock picking thing is separating the sheep

from the goats and it's always a good idea to let a machine do the boring work.

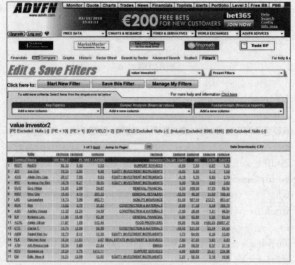

Sectors

Signal: Long

Difficulty: 4

The pros often talk about sectors. If you are a media company, you are in the media sector. If you have a mine, you are in the mining sector. Being in a sector usually means a company will trade in line with others in that group. Institutions look at sectors and decide if they are hot or not. This saves them a lot of time and means they can buy groups of companies for your pension rather than take a bits and bobs approach.

It makes a lot of sense. Apples are apples. Therefore, if you see a company in a sector whose valuation is way lower than a very similar company, you have to ask yourself why. Maybe there is no good reason.

In the old days, Orange's valuation was incredibly out of whack with Vodafone. Orange went up a lot and got bought out by French Telecom.

Of course Vodafone could have fallen, but other mobile companies had similar valuations, so Orange was the odd one out. In any event, if you wanted to be smart you could have shorted Vodafone and longed Orange and protected yourself from the outcome that Vodafone was too high instead of Orange being too low. This is called a hedge, the basis for the term 'hedge fund' (not that this is what they do these days).

You could look at Aer Lingus right now and wonder why it is valued so differently to Ryan Air or Easyjet. This differential was even bigger in the past before a 100% rise in Aer Lingus closed the gap somewhat (date of writing 18/9/10) but even so, the company's value still seems way out of whack.

So the game is to look at sectors and companies pretty similar to each other and see if one seems to be valued differently. If the companies are not too dissimilar, you should pay them some close attention.

Cash in the bank

Signal: Long

Difficulty: 4

Sometimes a company can have a ton of cash in the bank and sometimes it can be worth less than its bank balance.

Now it doesn't do to take this as a 'must buy' signal, as there may be, and probably is, something weird going on. Having said that it is worth taking a peek; often the company is just cheap!

However let's put that idea to one side.

A company angling up to go private will be moaning and groaning about how hard business is. They will do all kinds of things to make themselves look bad. Profits can be suppressed with accountants, all sorts of gimmicks can be used to make a set of books look bad, but one thing is hard to cover up: cash. For a start the company will want a pile of cash when it goes private because it won't be able to raise much of the market. It won't want to spend it or give it to creditors and it can't steal it in the traditional way. As such, when you look below the moaning and groaning, the cash will be growing.

Gotcha, you can think. Private Equity takeover on the way...

PEG, unleashed

Signal: Short

Difficulty: 6

We like P/E, which is a rather old measure of cheapness or otherwise. PEG is a turbo charged P/E; it has an added ratio thrown in to confuse. This added ratio is the rate of growth of profits.

This has the effect of moderating P/E for the rate of profit growth. If a company had a high P/E but was expanding like a plague of zombies, then this would lower the PEG, which is good. Likewise a company with a low P/E but a shrinking profit history would have a high PEG, thus showing it as a shaggy dog rather than a misunderstood pedigree.

PEG less than one = cheap, more than one = expensive.

This is a popular measure and a good one to throw into the mix. Like all tips and values it's a starting place rather than an absolute finishing line. However good a company looks, there can always be a good reason why it's a bad pick, and so a good going over is essential.

Dividends: cheques don't lie; except on the door mat

Signal: Short

Difficulty: 4

Dividends are great. The cheques that pop through the letter box are precious things. For a start no one can come and take them back, unlike the promises many companies make.

Dividends are living proof a company has at least the resources to cough up cash to its owners. This might seem like a trivial thing but it is actually a strong indication of a good business.

Many big companies have the sort of finances that would push families into bankruptcy court. Yet there are companies that make piles of money and these companies tend to pay dividends.

The City isn't much of a fan of dividends, mainly because of tax. A growing company that can plough back its cash into growing won't create a year dividend tax bill. Being able to plough back cash into growth should work out much better for shareholders in the long run. So goes the theory anyway.

However, a dividend from an unloved company is a good indication it's not about to go down the pan; what's more it's paying you out. Even big companies can be paying out over 5% of dividends, perhaps even 7 or 8%. That's a lot more than a government bond is paying, so the question is begged: is the company cheap? If a company paying a 5% dividend goes up 20% it will still be paying 4%, so a solid, high dividend-paying company has potential to rise under the pressure of its dividend payout.

The big downer—50% down from the high or more

Signal: Long

Difficulty: 7

We are looking to invest in what amounts to situations where the market is acting inefficiently. This is the equivalent of finding niches. Normal rules do not apply in niches and as such there are opportunities. For example, in the small cap end of the market there is value because the big boys can't play. This leaves opportunity for small fish.

If the market goes inefficient for whatever reason, prices go all over the map. It can be up too far in a bubble, it can be down too far in a crash. When the wheels come off, the market tends to lose its efficiency. In effect, the investor is looking for situations where things are broken and the market will pay them to fix them by participating.

When a stock falls heavily, the very fall itself can cause the market to seize up. This is an opportunity. As such, looking at stocks that have fallen over 50% is a good 'trash can' to go rummaging through. You can even look at shares that have dropped 70%, 90% or 99%!

The bigger the drop, the more enticing the opportunity can be. However, the market isn't that stupid. There has to be a good reason why a share has dropped 90% and there needs to be a very good one to make it fly again. You better be sure you know what that is and why everyone else is wrong. However, these opportunities do exist, even if they are rare.

This is not a mechanical signal; it is an invite to shovel tons of crud through your sluice box to find a golden nugget or two.

The less the fall, the greater the chance of resurrection and many stocks halve and double in a two year cycle. Therefore looking at stocks that have fallen around half is a more fertile group to search.

Stocks can fall a long way for no reason at all. They can fall because of the randomness of the market.

(Why? A random walk—think coin toss—will always bring you back to where you started, on average. But the furthest distance away from the starting point you will get to on your jiggly walk, on average, will go up with the square root of the number of coin tosses. So a randomly ticking share will wobble from its real price on a range that expands with the square root of its ticks. That's why a share can halve and double over the medium term yet go nowhere in terms of intrinsic value.)

So if a set of solid shares is wobbling about going nowhere you can follow their progress and pick up shares when they have wobbled far away from their value, on the basis that soon enough they will revert back to their origin. Clearly you have to keep tabs on a lot of stocks and keep up with their news, but in effect a lot of investors simply do just that; jumping in and out as a share judders around blown by random events. You can see that, in effect, investors are pushing shares back to their real values and the profit for this feeds the market's ability to offer the right price.

Rules of thumb

Investing isn't always by the numbers. The fuzzy world of words and politics are often more important than the gravity of finance. Ways 61-64 are about some of those fuzzy issues you need to keep an eye out for.

Don't play with political footballs

Signal: Short

Difficulty: 3

Industries and companies can become political footballs. When they do they are screwed. Business folk think they are smart and tough, but politicians are the next level of machismo. Politics will always crush business.

It is a happy business that operates away from the dead hand of government.

For sure, if an industry makes too much money, government will find a way to confiscate a lot of it.

One of the good things about new industries is that government takes a long time to get its fangs into them and therefore there is plenty of room for growth before the parasitical drain of government gets hold. The final phase of this death grip is when government tells business what to do and makes it pay for the blessing.

Now as a socialist you might be gung-ho for government; that's OK. Places with a lot of government and huge taxes like Sweden can certainly be better places to live than Puntland with neither tax nor government. However, as an investor, you invest in companies with an overlap with government at your peril.

If a company is actually a political football, it is doomed. A company caught up in a political process is like a ragdoll in a game of tug of war between two pit bulls. It can be fun to watch so long as you aren't the poor kid who owns the doll.

When politicians get involved in industry you need to remember; they don't know about business they know about politics. Politicians don't care about business, they care about politics. Politicians don't care about profits they care about politics. You get the idea.

As such, a company that gets itself caught in the political machine can expect to be horribly mangled.

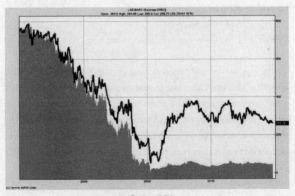

Barlcays v RBS

RBS (in grey) versus Barclays (in black). Perhaps a trifle unfair, but you get the idea. If only I could find my Railtrack chart!

Unhappy families

Signal: Short

Difficulty: 6

Picking shorts is a skill and of course the signs work as a way of disqualifying potential longs too. It's a good example of market symmetry.

Family firms are often brought up as fine examples of how business should be run. However in my experience you should never invest in a family firm.

Why?

There is a very simple reason: you are not part of that family. Blood is thicker than water and often the family will treat itself over and above the shareholders. Why do the sons of family founders get the CEO job when the old man retires—clearly because the kid, with his easy life so far, has utterly outperformed the rest of the world to win the top job? OK, so sarcasm is boring but I'm sure you follow the argument.

In history, the sons of great kings normally end up with their head on a spike. With business it's normally the shareholders that end up on the end of something nasty.

Hereditary management can't be in the interest of the nonfamily shareholders of a company, yet you would expect just that from a family firm and you can find it often.

Succession is of course the tip of the iceberg. Families tend to work in their own interests, which puts a family firm squarely into the category of a big fat risk.

To make matters worse, not only is blood thicker than water and the siblings no doubt thicker than the founder, when families fall out a lot of blood gets spilt. Time and time again family firms get in family feuds and mess up the business in the process.

In short, family firms are worth watching for their shorting potential. Many, especially small ones, will try to go private and not at a premium.

Old friends

Signal: Long

Difficulty: 5

If you have invested in a company just because you sold out, don't stop following it. The chances are, after you've sold, it will be painful to watch, as you see the profit you didn't make grow, or the loss you took disappear. Try to forget this. The random walk suggests that what happens next could go both ways on a 50/50 basis. This will make you a genius half the time and a fool the other half. Try to remember this.

The reason you are watching is because you have invested a lot of your time and effort in learning the facts on this business. That means you probably know more about the company than 99% of the City. You have this valuable expertise burnt to your brain. So as you keep a low level interest in the companies you have invested in you will occasionally see opportunity. This is in effect a second crop.

This is a particularly good technique during crashes. In a crash everything goes off a cliff. By having a data bank of old investments, you can pick up gems with a lot more confidence. You already know the horse you are going to ride and this lowers the risk of buying in at the riskiest of times.

Don't buy the top

Signal: Short (if you must)

Difficulty: 3

Why buy a share that has shot up a long way? Just don't do it.

This tip runs against a whole raft of investment advice. This advice is called momentum trading. In a nutshell it says: if it's hot, jump on it. My position is, just say no.

A share shooting up is not a sufficient reason to select it. There can be all kinds of traps set for people possessed to do that.

If you have a lot of nerve you can short this kind of situation as per *Broken mountain* (Way 23).

This would be the active thing to do, if you fancy the stress.

The passive thing is to just leave it alone. Don't buy a share that has risen a lot. How much of an optimist are you? OK, so in a Bull market this will work, but going long anything works in a Bull market.

If you are getting to the party late, just don't go. The greater fool theory of investing, which involves passing an overpriced share onto someone else before the inevitable crash occurs, relies on someone to hold the baby the very second everything craters. The later you get into a share that has zoomed up, the more likely you are to be that greater fool.

If you didn't see it early, you can't afford to buy it late.

Gold

A certain kind of investor loves gold. Do you love gold? You do!

For me it is just another metal. It isn't money. Its value, contra to a lot that is written, is very unstable. It is not a certain store of wealth.

It is not a hedge against inflation, not in the long run anyway. It is expensive and risky to hold.

It is a commodity like any other. Well actually it isn't, it is a commodity plus a large chunk of craziness.

Its uses are: electronics, teeth, trinkets and paying for big nasty wars.

I could write a book on this. It could make me rich as legions of gold bugs would buy it, just to laugh at it and burn it in the hearths of their survivalist retreats in mountains across desolate parts of America.

Several years ago I made a prediction that gold would hit $1000 an ounce and recently I moved that target to $2000. At the time of the first prophecy, the crowd asked whether I owned much and I said no, even though gold was around $400 at the time. They seemed amazed.

'Why not?'

I said I don't buy crazy stuff even if it is going up, because you have no sane basis to act on along the way.

I still hold to this in general, while I do have gold in my portfolio. Gold is, after all, a good thing to use for a splash of diversification; not that many gold bugs see it that way.

You just have to accept, to paraphrase, that gold is an irrational barbaric relic and people just love to play with it. That is OK but playing around with gold is not an investment strategy, it is speculation.

Let's not get physical: Gold ETF

Signal: Long

Difficulty: 1

If you want to buy gold, why not buy a gold ETF? We covered Stock Index ETFs earlier. Rather than buy a lump of gold which costs money to keep safely in a bank or lays in waiting in a sock in your home to be lost or stolen, you can buy a share which is an exchange traded fund and safely sits in your brokerage account.

The price of the share tracks the price of gold. OK you'll miss your pure animal pleasure of cuddling a Kruggerand or counting your sovereigns like scrooge, but at least it's safe from the marauding mob bound to form when paper money becomes worthless and hyper-inflation strikes. Oh dear I think I must have been visiting too many gold investment websites.

There are two gold ETFs currently in the UK: Gold Bullion (ADVFN ticker GBSS) or ETF Gold (ADVFN ticker BULP).

It's all the upside and none of the fun of holding the metal. If that alone puts you off you are not buying gold for the right reason.

Buy a gold producer

Signal: Long

Difficulty: 6

The trouble with holding gold or a gold ETF is that it goes up 1/1 with the gold price. You get no big bang leverage effect if gold booms. A lot of people who buy gold want to get rich when the world caves in and they want a multiplication of the impact of gold going up because they are sure the reckoning day is nigh. Gold mines can give you this extra upside.

Imagine a gold mine makes gold at $500 an ounce. The market price is $550 an ounce so they make $50 profit per ounce. When the gold price goes to $600 they are making twice as much profit an ounce and as such the company should be worth twice as much and its share price double. As such, when gold rises, the crummier the mine the more the share price will rocket.

A great mine with a low cost of gold will actually act more like a gold bar than a marginal mine because a rise in gold will have less affect on its profits than one hanging on with razor thin margins. Likewise, a fall will crush a marginal mine while leaving a rich mine much less affected by the gold price fall.

As such you need to dig into a mine's figures to work out what is going on. Gold mines are never simple.

A big thing to watch out for is hedging.

In the old days, a smart mine would sell its future gold production on the basis of a bird in the hand being worth two nuggets in the ground. This was a good move when the price of gold was going nowhere but down. Then the 20-year Bear market in gold reversed and suddenly mines had sold their gold production for years ahead, cheap. Darn!

Now many mines don't hedge their gold production and simply sell what they dig up. This is good news as long as gold rises. However, some mines still have hedges in place, or hedge some of their production; but not all. Locking in the selling price of your gold and getting a good night's sleep, instead of being speculators on tomorrow's price of gold is still a good idea, even if everyone thinks you are an idiot when you get it wrong.

A gold mine which has hedged its future productions will not rise with the price of gold. It has sold its golden eggs at a price in the past and now has to deliver them at that price until the end of the contract. This means that the mine isn't going anywhere much. Watch out for hedging or you can back the wrong mine; one without the zippy share price you crave.

Buy the 49ers

Signal: Long

Difficulty: 8

Now if you are a rabid gold bug, no risk is too big to take to ride the unstoppable gold tsunami. Gold is the only true money, the world economy is a vast elaborate fraud of printed valueless paper cash and soon only gold, soap and cigarettes will buy you those bullets you need to protect your desert compound from the mad max reality about to sweep civilisation away. Aheeem!

Anyway, even if that isn't you, you might want the maximum upside you can find to capture a big gold rally. The answer is to buy speculative gold mining exploration companies.

The trouble is these companies are REALLY speculative. Most have little more than a treasure map, a letter from a dodgy government to drill some holes in some remote backwater and small hope of hitting the big time. Of course if these companies do hit gold, their share price can go to the moon but, by and large, gold explorers are like horses that run races at the track: not a good way of making money.

BUT! When gold is going bonkers these mines fly. So if you wanted a maximum upside for a big Bull rally, you would buy a bag of speculative gold mines and while the market is hot you will do really well. People with Gold ETFs and boring gold producers will look longingly at your performance and sigh.

This is really only a tack for sophisticated investors who have watched this sector long and hard with a jaundiced eye. There are good spec mining companies out there among the Barnums of the mining world, but they are hard to differentiate.

The key is to not believe the hype when the strategy works. When gold hits $2000, don't believe the people that say it will hit $5000 or $10000 because most likely it won't. Instead, when the price turns and falls, your profits will go up in smoke at a tremendous rate. Be prepared to bail. If you don't get your timing right, the holders of gold ETFs and gold producers will look at your losses condescendingly and smile.

Gold has a silver lining

Signal: Long

Difficulty: 5

When gold goes up, so does silver. If you want to buy gold, by all means do, but you can buy silver too as a way of diversifying. You could also buy platinum and/or palladium shares because when gold goes up all the precious metals go up too; they are all elements with a high value. These are good ways of storing your money outside of currency. You can do this by investing in mines or ETFs. As diversification is a law you don't want to fight, use other precious metals to spread your risk; not only over type, but currency and geography. After all, there's no point buying a mine in a country if that country might go belly up in a financial, or political, disaster.

Let me give two examples of why, even with gold, diversification is a good idea. In the US at the bottom of the depression FDR confiscated—at coin face value—all privately held gold. The penalty for holding out was prison. Ouch! Gold is valued in US dollars, and in 2010 the value of the South African Rand was so high it was unprofitable for mines there to extract gold because their US dollar costs were so high.

Don't buy the gold mine, buy the spade maker

Signal: Long

Difficulty: 7

More tips on gold?

No, on general investing.

In many booms it seems that everyone wants to buy in. Consequentially prices are already high and the profits are slim. This happened in the Californian Gold rush where miners with bags of gold found a pint of beer or an apple cost a fortune. So much for the immutable value of gold. From this came the idea that the place to invest was not in gold miners and gold mines but in the people that sell buckets and spades and whiskey near mines. This is where the easy, real money is to be had.

This happened in the dotcom boom. It wasn't dotcom companies that ended up rich but the guys that sold databases and servers and network bandwidth and collocation facilities. These were the buckets and spades of that gold rush.

Likewise, if you think gold is going to rise strongly you might look to a refiner like Johnson Matthey who actually takes the raw output of a mine and refines it.

This of course works for any boom, craze or mania. Unlike the bewitched investors, don't buy the sizzle, buy the steak.

Meanwhile always remember the rule: up like a rocket and down like a stick.

What's up doc?

News drives markets. People are addicted to news and it often overwhelms share prices. Investors love news and you can harness it to make profits. Ways 70-83 are a few tricks to use the news to your advantage. It's the tip of the iceberg but it's a good place to start.

Sell tips

Signal: Short

Difficulty: 5

Tips are everywhere. Everyone loves to be told what share to buy. It is so much easier to buy a stock without any need to research or evaluate the company.

However, it is often the case that tips are promoted because someone wants to sell.

Magazine and newspaper tips are a good place to look for tips to SHORT or as a signal that a share you own is ready for selling.

Let's face it, most journalists are not financial gurus. The City is full of financial PR companies whose job it is to get a company written about and their success is not a reason to buy a share; in fact it turns out to be the opposite.

If you wanted to do this properly you would start various paper portfolios on a site like ADVFN and track the tipster tip for tip. Over time his performance will become apparent.

Pretty soon you will establish who is particularly weak.

A quicker way of doing this is to simply check out the stock and see if it is already a star performer, if it is, this could well be the end of the road.

This may just sound like the advice of a grumpy person, but there are a number of reasons why this works:

- A seller is drumming up PR to help them generate activity so they can sell into it, or perhaps raise money from an issue of stock.

- A stock has done so well that even a journalist can notice, so it is tipped on the basis that anything that has risen that far will go further. This is the vapid reasoning behind momentum investing.

- It's better to tip a favourite that everyone holds because they will like what they read and if it falls the tipster will be in good company.

- ...and finally, someone made it worth their while. God forbid!

When it hits the mainstream, it's over

Signal: Long or Short

Difficulty: 3

As a prolific journalist I should be less damning, but I have to say, if you read about it on the front page, whatever huge boom or bust that it is reporting is dead.

If the market is crashing and it's on the main news, the crash is very nearly over if not already on its way back up.

If you hear about a new investment craze you can be assured you have already missed it.

It used to be said if a taxi driver is talking about the market it's about to crash and when a waiter is tipping a stock it's time to sell. Today the equivalent of a taxi driver or bus boy is the mainstream news. This is why earlier I was talking about specialist press. The point is by the time the news percolates into the mainstream media—which is more interested in politicians' girlfriends and drug-snorting celebrities—the big brains in the tower blocks of the City have already stripped the kill to the bone.

However, if you are sitting in a crash and the papers are talking about the end of capitalism on their front pages, you can prepare to buy.

Likewise, if the media hasn't noticed something big is happening you might jump on for the ride.

If you hold gold and the media is saying it's going to $10,000 an ounce with a headline bigger than a declaration of war, you should get ready to sell.

Those reading this book near its publication date need only recall the recent Euro crisis and TV news shots of riots in the streets of Athens to know that once the media knows what's going on, it's already over.

Get rich slow, get poor quick

If you make 1% a day for four years you can turn $1000 into a billion. This is proof you can't get rich quick. To make higher returns you need to take higher risks and at some point risk of failure turns into certainty. This threshold is probably somewhere between 25-30% a year.

If you aim for more you are probably heading for disaster in the same way as standing closer and closer to the cliff edge increases you likelihood of falling off.

At 25% a year you will double your money every three years. 25% a year is a very tough target but one that is a good goal. Even at 10% money grows hugely over 20 years. So try for 25%, be happy with ten and build up a fat layer of wealth. If you try to double your money with every trade you won't be around for very long.

Think long-term, very long-term

Signal: Long

Difficulty: 4

While I keep saying get rich slow, no one is really interested in that idea. Because of this, ways of getting rich slow aren't followed much.

Getting rich slow ideas are macro trends.

If you can identify them you can invest in them now, early and at a low price.

For example, the gas drilling technique of 'fraking' has opened up untold natural gas reserves that only a few years ago were thought of as unrecoverable. 200 years of natural gas reserves makes the world a different place. All of a sudden the gas import terminals that were meant for gas importation for the Middle East are now used for exportation.

This is now a new game. Where are the profits to be had? Gas prices will fall. Lots of green tech looks expensive. Who has natural gas as a big input to their costs? Fertiliser manufacturers. Is there a big demand for more food? There sure is. Maybe with this macro trend in mind I might go looking for cheap fertiliser makers.

This is how you apply macro trends to picking stocks.

If you think people are going to get fatter, invest in plastic surgery equipment. If you think we are in for inflation, start tucking away the gold. If you build half a dozen long-term theories you can build a whole portfolio around that or simply use the idea to add a little extra interest or sparkle to your investing.

You can speculate and invest at the same time.

Read through

Signal: Long or Short

Difficulty: 7

An airline just released its profits; they are way down. It doesn't take a genius to guess other airlines are in trouble. Likewise an engineering company has a great year because the pound is weak and its products, which sell in dollars, are suddenly cheap or are making fatter margins. Again it doesn't take much brainwork to realise other engineers might be going great guns. This is called 'read through.'

Consequentially news about company A will affect company B in the same way.

Of course this can work both ways. If company A is a poor operation, company B will still fall but end up showing its superiority and recover.

So you can play read through both ways.

However, these days much of the trading that goes on is driven by correlation, that is to say how similar the movements of company A are to company B on a normal day. A fall in company A will drag down company B along these lines immediately. For traders this is a potential godsend because if they know the difference between the two they can jump on company B for a bit and let humans correct the mistake.

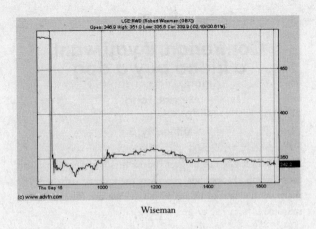

Wiseman

Wiseman and Dairy Crest are two dairies. Bad news from Wiseman hits Dairy Crest too. Dairy Crest recovers in the following hours.

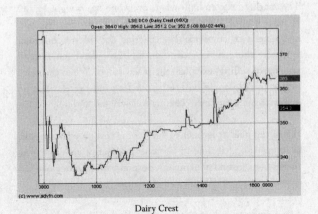

Dairy Crest

Contrarian: if you want a friend buy a dog

Signal: Long

Difficulty: 5

Some people say the market moves in a way that hurts the most people. People who have lost their shirt, and there are many, will relate to this (this is true but not for contrarian reasons).

Contrarianism works not because the market is evil but because of simple gravity. Here is the calculus:

The market is at its high when everyone has bought in and there is no one left to buy. Everyone is happy and excited, everyone is sat comfortably expecting the ride to continue, yet sadly there is no more fuel for the ride. Even a small amount of selling will push the price down. When the price begins to fall people will sell from fear and there still is no one with money to buy. The market will fall and fall.

When the market is desperately low, everyone who can sell, or must sell, has sold. Everyone is gloomy and dragging themselves around pouring out despondency, no one can sell anymore, they are OUT!

Any buyers that come along can't find willing sellers and with no one around to provide the stock they have to push prices up to get any. The rising price attracts buyers who push the price up. The price rises and generates more buyers and the price goes up and up.

LVMH bags are fashionable and expensive and flared jeans are out and cheap. This fact and the above is what drives contrarians.

So if you find a company in the dock, dustbin or on the shelf you can apply the other ways in this book to bolster your contrarian position.

Momentum: catch a rising star

Signal: Long

Difficulty: 8

Let's face it, you are not a contrarian. You like to buy into success. Your temperament means you're made to be a momentum investor. Few can resist the siren voices of momentum investing.

I could refuse to cover this as it's a lot trickier than people are led to believe, but it can work.

As always it has to be part of a broader strategy.

Let's say you've used some of the previous 'Ways' and this star fits them well and the share price is on its way to the moon. It is possible it could be one of your Macro trends and now folks are finally catching onto it. A momentum investment doesn't have to be pure crazy speculation, even if it often is.

Big trends like tech in the '90s and mining over the last few years can run and run, so momentum investing is not a total death trap. However, it is dangerous as once you are simply trading what the herd is charging at you have lost your rational compass. That compass is important.

Apple is the perfect case for a momentum stock and in their day so were Microsoft, AOL and Google. You could feel the crowd willing them on. These companies were rock stars and Apple still is.

There was as lot of money to be made from these companies' supernatural rises and who knows the fate of Apple (I say down!).

If you see a big company with a huge fan base, then you can consider following it but don't become a fan yourself. Use as many of the 'Ways' as possible and try not to catch the almost unavoidable comeuppance.

Apple Incorporated

Good luck Mr Jobs.

New brooms

Signal: Long

Difficulty: 7

If you follow a company for a long time you get a feeling for the management. Often it is less than brilliant. This won't be great for the share price. Consequentially when that management goes, there is a chance good things can start to happen.

However much a CEO and his board like to think they are smart, a business that is established can run for long periods of time on autopilot and the resultant decline can be slow and invisible. At some point the dam breaks, all hell breaks loose and the management is replaced. The only way to see this at work is to look closely at the financial reports and try to judge the quality of the profits and assets.

The new management might be great. Normally their previous track record will give you a hint on several levels. Here are some pointers:

a) They did well before and will do well again.

b) They came from a good place. Who would board a sinking ship? Perhaps there is life in the old dog yet.

c) They talk sense, even in the past or on joining.

d) You can imagine that they might be brought in to sell off the company.

If the new management is good versus previous management being poor, this is a good long-term sign and you should go long. This is especially true of a solid established business.

However, the reverse is also true; a hot new company with hot management replaced with dud new bosses can kill a company. You need to watch out for this too.

New brooms
and 'kitchen sinking'

Signal: Long

Difficulty: 7

Good new management is a good sign, and a radical approach to the balance sheet is also a good tip off.

New management wants to appear great. So when it moves in, it organises its accountants to write off every possible asset they can (this side of legality). As the previous management will have been desperately trying to paint over the cracks, this process will throw out all the bad news in one go and rack up a single gigantic loss. These will be blamed, in implied fashion, on the old guard, now gone.

This process is called kitchen sinking, as in 'throwing everything in, including the kitchen sink'.

Kitchen sinking will give the new management a clean sheet on which to write profits. It will probably batter the share price in the short-term too, which can be a good point to buy.

Kitchen sinking is good for several reasons. The first is, this management is demonstrably hard-nosed and ruthless. An ailing company needs that. Secondly, it will now be very easy to manufacture good results going forwards as all the crap in the balance sheet is gone and some vague assets can probably be rolled back in later too.

For some odd reason, the City doesn't seem to recall that a year earlier the new management 'kitchen sinked' their results. The City is only interested in what is under their noses today—that is a fat improvement in profit by the new guys in charge. This will help make the share popular going forwards and the company's share price will experience a renaissance.

As such, tough kitchen sinking by new management is a good way to pick out a share to research.

Check the website

Signal: Long or Short

Difficulty: 4

The website will tell you a lot about the management, explicitly and implicitly. Many companies even have photos of the management. These can be truly grim, but the point of looking at the website is to evaluate the general personality of the company and look for clues of quality or otherwise.

I will illustrate this with an example.

I was interested in a mine in a faraway desert.

On the website it showed the mine and work in progress.

The management were in a few shots of the mine, and its workers under the desert sun. Their faces were as white as a Scottish office worker's. Clearly they didn't spend much time at the mine.

The equipment was impressive, but it seemed unscratched and dusty. The big trucks still had paint inside the load-carrying tipper bays. Clearly not many tonnes of rock had been ferried about.

Whoever had put together the website hadn't been briefed on the official story.

You shouldn't invest in a company which has a website full of wishful thinking. Likewise, a good website is a positive indicator.

Every dark hurricane cloud has a silver lining

Signal: Long

Difficulty: 3

You would have thought insurers would hate disasters—after all it costs them. Not a bit of it, they love them.

Insurers love a catastrophe because it is an excuse for them to jack up their prices. It is a price fixing collusion that requires no dodgy meetings. They all know what to do when disaster strikes. They all bang up their premiums.

Of course an earthquake or hurricane today does not increase or decrease the likelihood of one tomorrow so when they have gouged the market for higher premiums, insurers proceed to make bumper profits.

So when disaster strikes, you buy insurers.

It's simple, it's dumb, but it works.

Of course don't just buy any insurer, do lots of research; it won't hurt to pick the best one.

Buy rumour, sell fact

Signal: Long or Short

Difficulty: 6

This is an old investing maxim. It's good for traders. A trader will latch onto the undertow of a rumour and sell out just before the confirmation or otherwise of it. That's fun if you like to trade.

An investor isn't really that interested unless, of course, a rumour has driven the company he has invested in to a point he feels like taking his profit. Some investors like to have set profit-taking points, say 30%; some hold on forever while others let their profits run and then jump out when they get the flutters.

If a piece of good news triggers your selling goal, then it is a good time for an investor to cash out as, time after time, it is the secret unreleased news that drives the price, with the hard news at the end of the road for the rise itself. Unless there is something else working away; after everyone knows the story, there is nothing to come to push the price up.

Browse and research

Signal: Long

Difficulty: 4

You simply cannot know all stocks and you cannot hope to get your head around everything that is happening. You can also not hope to pull a model of the markets out of thin air. There is no better way to find stocks to pick than by browsing around the internet.

Clearly you don't want to do this at random, but a financial site like ADVFN, or any one of a number, should be the base for you to set out into the world of the internet in search of fact and consequence.

An investor is basically a judge. They judge a company on its merits using knowledge. Most of that knowledge is out there already, you just have to go and find it and assemble the jigsaw.

Because most investors want to be told, be they professionals in search of research or private investors hungry for tips, any investor that actually hones their knowledge will be streets ahead of the competition.

This slowly built advantage is the basis for how you pick stocks and get rich slow. Relying on others is by far the riskier path.

Look for history repeating itself

Signal: Long

Difficulty: 4

The market is just the average take on the value of stocks at the time of consideration. If you averaged the participants into one person, it would probably be a well paid fifty-year-old with grey hair and a love of claret.

Just like a football crowd sings with one voice the market trades with one too and as the generations rotate, history repeats itself.

It doesn't take much hindsight to see we have just relived the seventies.

We have had an oil shock, a Middle East war, a stock market crash, a banking crisis, a rubbish Labour government, a commodity boom; the list goes on. If you had spotted this you would have done well over the last few years.

There is no punk rock but there's emo. OK, so safety pins through your nose is now a diamond pin through your cheek, but it is the same cycle, just in a slightly different order.

This of course could be a mad point of view, but as I write inflation is coming, austerity and economic rebuilding is on the horizon; does that seem late '70s or early '80s to you?

My point is, watch for the repeating cycles and get in early. The dotcom boom will come again. This is maybe ten years out, but when it strikes you should already be in on the ground floor. It might not be computers, it might be robots, but it will be similar and resonant of 1995-2000. Then, if you are still going in 2030, watch out for those banks going belly up!

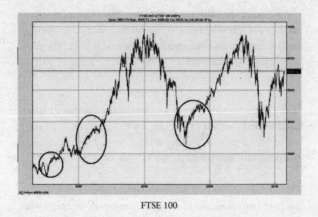

FTSE 100

This is the FTSE 100. On top of the highlighted patterns, you can match up the corrections between one rally and the next. The two big cycles are spookily similar.

Long-term earnings growth

Signal: Long

Difficulty: 7

A good company can grow and grow. This is a rare company but one definitely worth owning. What could be better than buying a share and watching it mushroom over 20 years? Take a look at Microsoft or Apple's history and you will see what long-term growth can do.

Using FilterX you can pull up companies that have already achieved long-term growth and you can dig down and see if it can have a shot at keeping it up. If it can then it's a great candidate to add to your portfolio.

This is how Warren Buffett, the guru king of investment, made his vast fortune. He bought companies that were well run that could grow and grow over the long-term, then sat back and left it to them to make him rich.

These companies are rare but worth the effort to find. Obviously we'd all like to be as rich as Warren Buffet. Most people, however, can't abide the boredom of it. Don't let getting rich in your sleep put you off.

What's up officially doc?

RNS is the official market news. RNS is like general news but on steroids. Here are a few ways to use the RNS which can be found on the internet on sites like ADVFN.

Directors' buys

Signal: Long

Difficulty: 4

Directors' buying is a classic tip off that a company is cheap. A director's buy or sell of stock must be announced in the RNS (regulatory news) which can be found on ADVFN.

Directors obviously know a thing or two about their business. Things like: the skeletons in the cupboard, the condition of the market, the long-term strategic plan, the skills of the other directors, the likelihood of a takeover etc. They know stuff that no one else can possibly know. So when they buy their own stock the chances are good the company is worth a look.

Company directors aren't always stinking rich, so putting a few thousand pound into the company's shares is not going to be taken lightly. Like most people, their expenditure is likely to meet their incomings, so the investment is probably real.

However, this investment idea is not novel and some directors will buy to try and encourage other investors to follow suit. The thing to do is look back over the RNSs and see if they bought shares in the past and what happened next. If they buy and the price falls it's worth thinking twice.

Likewise a cheap company where the directors aren't buying is a bit of a turn off, but like share sales by directors there can be good reasons for this. However, selling or not buying should be born in mind.

If a company fits a lot of your selection criteria, then all systems are go!

Because directors' buys are easy to follow (for example ADVFN has a special page tracking them) it can be a good jumping off point in your research. Spot a buy, then check out the rest of the info; it's a handy and quick way to do your homework.

Management competence: throwing parties in breweries

Signal: Long

Difficulty: 6

Reading year end and interim reports and company updates will tell you a lot about the management.

A company is very dependent on its management. You would hope so, seeing how well it is paid. However, in this rather random world we live in there are all shades of management from criminal at one end to saintly at the other; alright, maybe not saintly. Even so, all managements are not equal.

As such, you should look very carefully at the management of the business.

You should use statements by the company to the market as a kind of written interview.

If you like the cut of the CEO and Chairman's jib, then it's a good signal that this might be a stock for you. If the management statement gives you the creeps, you should avoid the company like the plague.

For me, I'm cautious when a company starts its statements… 'I'm delighted to announce this year's figures, which show an increased loss for the year up by…' Delighted by an increased loss?

I am not sure where the delight comes from. Maybe it is getting their interesting numbers passed the auditor at all that produces the delight. In any event I always look out for oddness in reports; oddness is a poor indicator.

You'd think I was joking until you spent a few minutes checking year end statements.

If you go back over the years you can also read the company's updates to the market. Do the optimistic statements of new deals turn into sales? You would be amazed at companies who tell the market about a never ending flow of deals yet never seem to have any sales subsequently; even after several years. Often these companies are keen to pump up the share price and are very popular with investors because of it, but you should avoid getting suckered in.

Use what the management writes to benchmark its quality. Look for good clear statements one year that are followed through with results in the next. The story of the company should flow with the times and make sense. If it does then it's thumbs up, if not then thumbs down.

RNS alert

Signal: Long or Short

Difficulty: 7

Most RNS are released before market open or after market close. However in some cases it is released during the day.

This kind of news will move the market a long way.

If you are fast enough you can jump on a rise before it's finished.

As such, it's a good idea to keep your eye on it.

Conversely, if a share suddenly takes off to the moon during the day and there is no RNS, chances are a rumour has hit the market; something like a false takeover story. If the cat is out of the bag, the company must respond. The more time that elapses after the price spike without any news, the more likely there is no cat and no bag and the rumour is false.

As a trader you can sit and wait and as soon as enough time has elapsed, it becomes increasingly unlikely the rumour is true. When the price starts to fall away you can short the share and ride the price down.

It's fun, it's dangerous and it's profitable, but it's strictly for traders who want to sit by a screen all day long.

'The next big thing'

Signal: Long

Difficulty: 6

If you watch the news long enough you will pick up on 'the next big thing.' Small companies in particular are floated because there is investor appetite for that kind of business, not because the company needs to be public. Many flotations are in themselves opportunistic. By watching the news you can see what the City thinks is hot as an idea. This is why all of a sudden the market will be full of new internet casinos or rare earth element exploration companies.

When you spot this trend you can look to jump on the wave by buying already established companies in the sector.

As suggested in Way 31 you can do the same in the US. If the US markets are floating dental companies en masse, pick up dental companies in the UK and wait. 'The next big thing' is normally a wave that lasts a year or two, so catching it early can add a nice pep to your portfolio.

Like all fashion-based investments, do not end up believing the hype. Remember shares are financial instruments not football teams.

Mad management

Signal: Short

Difficulty: 4

Apparently 2.5% of the population is certifiably mad. On that basis, 50 companies in London have a mad CEO and 50 a mad finance director. One listed company should, according to statistics, have both.

You should seriously consider shorting a company where the management seems mad. It might seem unlikely, but you will nonetheless come across instances where you cannot come to any other conclusion. A quick recap of the credit crunch throws up any number of candidates.

Likewise, when important managers resign because of 'stress', you can be quite sure nothing good is going to happen to the company.

Profit warnings

Signal: Short

Difficulty: 5

Companies really hate to announce profit warnings. Companies get their share price badly smashed if they release one. As such, companies try to avoid them and this often means that when they are forced to come clean the news is so bad they can't release all of it at the same time.

This is why profit warnings are said to be like buses, if you see a profit warning, two or three are liable to be close behind.

The thing to watch for is a lack of clarity in the first warning. If it isn't forthright and doesn't say, 'this is definitely all you need to know, there is no further bad news' and instead says: 'the management is evaluating developments' more bad news is bound to follow.

A profit warning, especially for a business with lots of debt, can be the beginning of the end.

If the warning slips something in at the end that sounds harmless but uses weasel words pay close attention. This is where the indications of what happens next are hidden. A vague line about discussions with the company's bankers is all you normally need to know that the profit warning is just the beginning of the trouble.

Oil

Oil is like gold, a fascinating area for investors and speculators. It's a risky place to play but people can't keep away. As such, it's good to have a selection of tricks up your sleeve.

Buy an oil producer

Signal: Long

Difficulty: 7

Some people like gold; some can't get enough of oil. It is kind of a similar addiction.

The choices are the same. You can buy an ETF, which is better than having a tank of petrol in your garage and way safer. The ADVFN tickers for them are LSE: OILG and LSE: OILS. The ETFs also include oil with gas and buying gas in the same stock shouldn't put you off, if you want naked exposure to hydrocarbons.

Then you can buy shares in the producers such as Shell or BP and you can also buy an ETF that rolls up a bunch of US oil producers into one share. On ADVFN you can find them under the following tickers: LSE:0o41 and LSE:0o42.

There are, of course, huge oil companies in the UK like Shell and BP and a host of US and European oil companies to boot, but the thing to remember is that oil companies don't own oil; governments own oil.

Oil companies are simply hired hands who do all the work and take all the risk, while governments take the lion's share. This is not an anti-government rant, it's just a fact. You only need to look at the tax on a gallon of petrol to see that at work.

The trouble is because of this, oil can zip all over the place in price and not really affect an oil company like Shell. However, blow up a drill hole in the sea and your share price could sink with it; as BP found out.

That aside, oil companies pay fat dividends and it's probably a reflection of the risk inherent in owning an oil company that their P/E is so low and their dividends are so high.

So if you want oil, you need to really stretch to combine ideas. Contrarian plus oil might equal BP, dividend plus oil might equal Shell. One thing is for sure—oil companies are big and, in a way, you need a little oil in your portfolio to be diversified, but don't buy big oil if you want to make big bucks on a spike in the oil price.

Those darn wildcatters

Signal: Long

Difficulty: 8

Like the gold explorers, the oil exploration companies will do extremely well, if you pardon the pun, when oil shoots up. For a start, expensive oil gets viable when prices rise. What is un-commercial at $40 a barrel is suddenly amazingly profitable at $90. Also a 50/50 prospect of $50 a barrel oil is a lot more valuable as oil rises. Even a tall story about oil in faraway places becomes more valuable as the price of crude rises.

It is insanity, however, to put a lot of money into a single oil explorer; it is equivalent to financial suicide. At best you should put a little money into many, separating the ultra-dodgy from the plausible.

Chuck out any explorer that has management from previous failures; discard any company that leaves you scratching your head about what they are going on about and avoid companies involved with any litigation or any dodgy sounding complicated deals. OK that won't leave you many companies but don't say I didn't warn you.

Once again remember, 'shares that go up like a rocket, go down like a stick.'

Vorsprung durch technik

Investing can get technical. Technical issues in the market leave most people cold or confused. As such, grasping some of the technicalities can add to your profits. 92-100 are a few opportunities to get you started. You can't know too much in investing.

Trading costs;
the less the better

Signal: Long or Short

Difficulty: 3

Do not give your profits to your broker or the market. They do not deserve them.

Costs are often hidden and you should understand them.

If you buy a small cap with a spread of 95-100 (that's 95 to sell and 100 to buy) you lose 5p or 5% just buying and selling.

A £10 a trade online broker giving you this as an automatic trade is a very expensive broker indeed. My broker Derek at TSCtrade would probably get me the stock at 98 and sell it at 96 by ringing up the market maker and doing a deal. That's a 3% saving that amounts to £150 on every £5000 of stock. He is therefore much cheaper, even at a commission of 0.75% than a flat rate £10 a trade broker.

Understand your costs and keep them low; the savings compound over time. Likewise, put your shares in an ISA. Over the years, the tax savings will have a huge impact, because at some point you will hit Capital Gains Tax (CGT) and that hurts your returns badly.

Costs are often hidden. CFDs and spread bets, for example, have a built-in finance cost so, when you leverage £1000 up to £10,000 to buy a stock, you pay, say, 7% finance on the £10,000; that is £700 a year or 70% of your capital. Imagine the share simply doesn't move for a year. That's expensive even if you are dealing for free.

Spend some time understanding your costs and then keep them in check.

Sell in May and go away. Summer holidays at work

Signal: Long

Difficulty: 4

Firstly, you should not sell in May and buy back in September. This can be an expensive mistake even if the market falls during this period. The exact timing of when it falls and when it bounces is almost impossible to gauge. Get it wrong and you get the fall and then miss the bounce. This can be horrendously disappointing and costly.

However, the summer is increasingly quiet these days and the market often feels like it has ground to a halt.

Stocks therefore seem to have a tendency to fall away in the summer, so a good technique is to hold off buying stocks you fancy, which are falling, until they have reached a bottom.

The way to do this is by putting on a trailing alert which says: alert me when this stock goes up from its low. This way, as it continues to fall or flails around, you sit back and wait, but when the trend reverses and some zip is back in the stock and it rises say 5%, you get an email saying, 'come look'. Then you make the choice of whether to buy or not. You can get alerts like these on websites but of course I use the ADVFN system, as in my biased opinion it is the best.

The trader of course can feel free to trade the Bearish

environment knowing that the chances of a crash or correction are heightened by the lack of summer action.

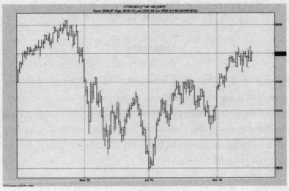

FTSE 100

They certainly sold in May 2010! But by September you are back to square one. Sell in late April and buy back in the summer? Shame that doesn't rhyme.

The Santa Effect

Signal: Long

Difficulty: 5

Shares tend to rally at Christmas. This is because it is year end and two things happen: funds with risky strategies, often involving short positions, close out so they can go off on holiday early, and standard fund managers buy stocks they own to spike them for the year end and, thereby, show better returns than they deserve.

Of course nothing works 100% of the time and a bad market will overcome all technical moves like this. However, in mediocre years the Santa Effect has appeared very frequently.

So for a trader it is a good trend to watch for and be ready to jump on board. A FTSE future or FTSE Tracker or spread bet would be ideal ways to ride along with the reindeer.

Close of day auction

Signal: Long

Difficulty: 8

Most investors haven't even heard of auctions. Yet at the beginning and the end of each trading day there is a share auction to open or close the market where in a five minute period traders and investors can put bids in for stocks. At the end of the process the result is worked out and the bidders either do or don't get their orders filled. It is an exciting and often confusing event.

In volatile times, these prices can go a bit crazy.

In say a crash or a bubble, or in periods of corrections or other such abnormality, these auctions are worth watching as you can pick up bargains. Auctions can go haywire in turbulent times and this brings opportunity.

Just before the auction is over you can put in bids and hope to get cheap stock. You can also short a stock that has suddenly jumped up.

This is a game for the brave and patient and it is definitely only for traders. However, it doesn't cost to watch and learn.

(chart overleaf)

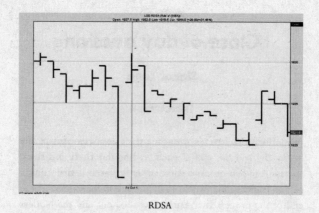

RDSA

Even a Big Cap like Shell can react to the limited window of an auction.

Way 96

No news but it's moving

Signal: Long

Difficulty: 4

A company that is rising or falling without any news is a share to watch. You can spot a company like this from Directors' Buys, Top gainers, Break outs, a Bulletin Board or any number of ways.

The point is the share is going somewhere without any reason, or at least any reason which is known in the public domain. The best ones are the quietest ones; the ones that move without volatility or suddenness. A determined ticking up over an extended period is like a float twitching to a fisherman.

This is cause to go off and start digging.

Big gains

Signal: Long

Difficulty: 5

It is a good idea to watch the list that shows today's big gainers. For the trader it's a signal to jump on a fast moving stock; whether that's to jump on the trend or try and catch its turn.

The bigger the move, the better for a trader.

For an investor the big gainers list can show two things: what is hot and in vogue, and how what was once a dead stock is back in action. The first is useful for trying to find an equivalent share that hasn't moved, and the latter to see if a sleeping beauty is about to rise and shine.

The big gainer list, popular on sites like ADVFN, will have a heavy contingent of what the market thinks is exciting. For instance, as I write, there will be lots of mines on the list. The hot sector is always worth keeping an eye on. Opportunities will arise and consistent big risers and fallers are worth a look, just to see if there is any real value in the company.

There will also be a fair number of broken companies jumping about in their death throes. Ignore these. They have tiny share prices and a few buys can make them shoot about. However, they are untradeable, below investment quality and a waste of time and money.

There will also be dormant companies with good businesses who are sparking back into life. If you see one of these you may want to add it to your portfolio.

Percentage gainers lists, like directors' buys, are a good platform to alert you to prospects. It is a starting place, not a green light in itself.

Breakouts

Signal: Long

Difficulty: 5

Shares trading in a trend tend to stick in that channel. Every time the price looks like it's about to jump into new territory it is highly likely to drop back off. This is the basis for swing trading. However due to market symmetry there is no certainty this will happen. One time out of five it will break out and then possibly go way higher.

This is also the basis for the Box system of Way 19. A good way to find companies breaking out is to use an ADVFN 'Top List' called Breakouts.

A favourite is a 52 week break out or down which shows companies breaking highs or lows of the year. This is a particularly interesting breakout as it is watched by traders who believe it to be very important. They think it's important because the media likes to talk about highs and lows of the year and therefore 52 weak break outs can get attention from the herd.

As always this is a good place to start your research, the more 'Ways' that fit the situation, the better.

Constant gainers

Signal: Long or Short

Difficulty: 4

A company that keeps sneaking up every day is a no brainer to consider for your portfolio. Someone is clearly buying and you'd hope that would be for a reason.

Constant Gainers is a particularly useful 'Top List' on ADVFN.

This list contains companies that have been going up day after day; from three days in a row up to as many days in a row as there are. In a good market some companies can rise for two or three weeks in a row.

A good one to look for is a share that is inching up, rather than zooming. Not that zooming up is bad, it is just that a company that is being snaffled up sneakily is more sexy than some shooting star on its firework trajectory.

When you look at the stock's chart, if it is going up steadily without much volatility this is a super candidate for you to examine further. A lack of volatility is a sign of certainty and purpose.

You can of course turn this on its head and look for constant fallers. This too will work well for a Bear. A slow consistent fall is the sign of someone big easing themselves out of a large position. This is blood in the water for a Bearish shark or even a sharkish Bear.

Re-examine your portfolio

Signal: Long

Difficulty: 4

If you are investing correctly you have lots of stocks in your portfolio and some are doing great and some aren't.

Take a look at the dogs and think: is the reason I bought in still good? How does this stock look now? If it has fallen, perhaps drastically, yet it still fits your criteria and it still feels right, consider picking up more.

You can't time the market and just because you bought doesn't mean it's going up right away. It's where the stock is in a couple of years you are interested in. Even then you will have your winners and losers, but you never know specifically which is which. It's just that your overall return is good, because you have been diligent and careful.

With this in mind you should look at your current portfolio occasionally and decide if you want to buy more, while at the same time considering whether to sell out others.

Your portfolio is after all your most understood and researched selection and as such the safest zone to pick from. Yet remember to keep diversified; don't get overweight in any one stock however keen you are on it.

Use all available tools

Signal: Long

Difficulty: 4

There are over 2,000 stocks in the UK. Their size goes from a total value of £300,000 to £118 billion. You can make as much money from the tiddler as the giant.

The thing about the market is you make a decision, contact your broker and you are either right or wrong. There is no thief in the night, no saboteur, no voodoo to thwart you, just the tough job of picking the right shares to buy and looking after them properly.

When you are going to buy a stock, do not just use a signal to do so. Use your half dozen favourites. Make sure your selection process has as many cross references as you can.

Obviously a stock can't fit all criteria, especially when there are a 101 in this book, but they can certainly fit half a dozen.

I take my favourites, look at a list of prospects and mark each stock out of 10 for each value I'm on the look out for.

I add up the scores and then I pick the top stock. There is no need to dive headlong into any investment; there are always new stocks tomorrow.

You will always be unlikely to pick the sexiest stock of the year and you will probably pick a number of stocks that will go bust. Yet because you have a diverse portfolio it will all come out in the wash.

As you weight your selections by your favourite 'Ways' you will build up skill in applying your rules and you will build up general knowledge in the market.

The process of evaluation will build up your ability to make better returns.

It is common sense.

The market will pay you to invest and help you get rich slow.

If you treat the market like a farm it will give you a crop. If you want to treat it like a casino it will deal with you like a gambler.